The Bride's Cook Book

by

Douglass Publishing Co.

APPLEWOOD BOOKS
Bedford, Massachusetts

The Bride's Cook Book

was originally published in

1909

ISBN: 978-1-4290-1021-4

Thank you for purchasing an Applewood book.
Applewood reprints America's lively classics—
books from the past that are still of interest
to the modern reader.
For a free copy of
a catalog of our
bestselling
books,
write
to us at:
Applewood Books
Box 365
Bedford, MA 01730
or visit us on the web at:
For cookbooks: foodsville.com
For our complete catalog: awb.com

Prepared for publishing by HP

THE BRIDE'S COOK BOOK

"A HAPPY HOME IS A JOY FOREVER"

We may live without poetry, music and art;
We may live without conscience, and live without heart;
We may live without friends; we may live without books;
But civilized man cannot live without cooks.

"*Lucile*"

PRICE $1.00

THE DOUGLASS PUBLISHING CO.
MONTGOMERY BLOCK
SAN' FRANCISCO, CAL.

A FEW HINTS ON HOW TO START A DAY.

A lady's taste and nicety are very perceptible at the breakfast table. She should never allow a soiled tablecloth to appear on it. The linen should be fresh and snowy white, the tea, coffee, or cocoa, nicely made, and, if possible, fresh flowers and fruit should adorn the table. A nicely laid, pretty, appetizing breakfast is a great promoter of good temper and harmony through the ensuing day. A soiled tablecloth, tough, cold toast, weak tea, bitter coffee, etc., are enough to derange both the temper and digestion of those who have to submit to such domestic inflictions. Let our homes be bright, sunny, and charming; and that such may be the case, open the day with a cheery and well arranged breakfast table.

The Bride's Menu.

Blue Points.

Queen Olives.

Canape of Anchovies.

Consomme.

Baked Halibut.

Potatoes Hollandaise.   Cucumber Salad.

Sweetbread Pates.

Fried Spring Chicken.

French Peas.   Lettuce.   Asparagus.

Pudding Diplomatique, Sauce Duchesse.

Tutti Frutti Ice Cream.

Black Coffee.   Cheese.

Nuts.

Assorted Fruit.

Canape of Anchovies—Cut toast in triangles, chop anchovies fine, spread on toast and sprinkle with chopped hard boiled eggs.

Potatoes Hollandaise—Boil plain kidney potatoes; dress with the following sauce: Three yolks of eggs, half a cup vinegar and water, beat up in a double boiler until it thickens, add a tablespoon of melted butter and season to taste with a little lemon juice, pepper and salt.

Cucumber Salad

Sweetbread Pate

Pudding Diplomatique—Take a pudding mold greased well with butter. Take a layer of sponge cake, then a layer of chopped pineapple, add another layer of cake then a layer of quartered Maraschino cherries, and so on until the mold is filled, then make custard as follows and pour over the cake: To four ounces of sugar mixed with six eggs, add one quart milk, a pinch of salt and lemon flavor. Bake in a medium oven.

Sauce Duchesse—Take apricot marmalade thinned with Kirschwasser and white wine, serve hot with pudding.

Tutti Frutti Ice Cream—Chopped glace fruit, figs and nuts thoroughly mixed with vanilla ice cream.

Here Are Medicinal Foods.

Watercress is an excellent blood purifier.

Lettuce has a soothing effect on the nerves and is excellent for sufferers from insomnia.

Tomatoes are good for a torpid liver, but should be avoided by gouty people.

Celery is a nerve tonic; onions also are a tonic for the nerves.

Spinach has great aperient qualities and is far better than medicine for sufferers from constipation.

Beetroot is fattening and good for people who want to put on flesh.

Parsnips possess the same virtues as sarsaparilla.

Cranberries correct the liver.

Asparagus stimulates the kidneys.

Bananas are beneficial to sufferers from chest complaints.

Celery contains sulphur and helps to ward off rheumatism.

Honey is a good substitute for cod-liver oil.

The juice of a lemon is excellent for sore throat, but should not be swallowed, but used as a gargle.

Carrots are excellent for gout.

BREAKFAST DISHES.

Coffee.

For three cups, take three tablespoonsful of the finest mixed Mocha and Java, mix the coffee with one egg in a dish; when thoroughly mixed, pour into the coffee pot containing cold water and bring to a boil. THEN YOU HAVE COFFEE.

Chocolate.

Time, ten to twelve minutes.—Scrape up about a quarter of a pound of a chocolate cake into saucepan with two gills of water; set it on the fire; stir it constantly with a wooden spoon until it is rather thick, then work it very quickly with the spoon. Stir in a pint of boiling milk by degrees and serve it.

Cocoa.

Time, five hours.—A quarter of a pound of cocoa nibs to three quarts of water, to be boiled down to two quarts and a half. The nibs to be strained after five hours' boiling. If they are allowed to remain in the cocoa, it becomes bitter and unpalatable.

Oatmeal Porridge.

Time, half an hour.—Put a pint of warm water into a stewpan over the fire, and as it boils dredge in two ounces of oatmeal with your left hand, and stir with the right. When it is made, turn it into a soup-plate, adding a little salt or a little sugar, according to taste. Send it to table with a jug of hot milk, which should be added to it by degrees for eating.

Breakfast Mush.

To make a breakfast for four persons, take about one pint of creamery mush and stir boiling water into it to the consistency desired (salted to suit the taste), cook about five minutes, serve with cream and sugar. Fresh or stewed fruit added will make a delightful breakfast.

If any mush is left over from breakfast, after it becomes cold cut in slices and fry for another meal.

Omelette.

Take four eggs and beat as light as possible. For every egg add a tablespoonful of milk. Put a piece of butter in the omelette pan, and when hot pour in the mixture. With a fork scrape the egg very lightly toward the center of the pan as it cooks, and when done fold it together with a pancake turner.

How to Boil Eggs.

Put the eggs into cold water, place on the range and as soon as the water comes to a boil they are thoroughly cooked, not from the outside in, but from the inside out, a few moments now will boil them suitable for salad dressing or sandwiches.

Poached Eggs.

Have boiling water in a shallow pan, break the eggs separately in a saucer, and slip gently into the boiling water; when all are in the water, place the pan over the fire until the white of each is perfectly set; remove with a slicer and lay on buttered toast or broiled ham.

Baked Eggs.

Time, eight minutes.—Have a little beef fat in the tin, let it be hot, then break in the eggs as for frying; salt them and set in hot oven for a few minutes and they are done. Eat with buttered toast.

Egg and Oyster Omelette.

Time, twelve minutes.—Beat up four eggs, and season to suit; chop up six large oysters, make a batter of a half cup of flour and a half pint of milk; mix the whole together, stir well, and fry slowly, adding by the teaspoonful.

Scrambled Eggs.

Beat up four eggs, with salt and pepper to taste. Put an ounce of butter into a saucepan; directly it is melted put in the eggs, and keep constantly stirring with a spoon until they are nearly set, adding at the last a little finely-minced parsley.

Breakfast Baked Omelette.

Time, fifteen minutes.—One heaping teaspoonful of corn-starch, one-fourth cup of milk, a lump of butter, a small onion chopped fine; boil all together until the corn-starch gets thick—not lumpy—take seven eggs, beat the yolks and whites separately—the whites to a stiff froth; put the corn-starch in a dish with the yolks and half cup of milk, add a little salt and pepper, some chopped parsley, lastly the whites of the eggs. Bake fifteen or twenty minutes in a hot oven.

Milk Bread.

Time, one hour.—One pint of boiling water, one pint of new milk, one teaspoonful soda, the same of salt, flour enough to form a batter; let it rise, add sufficient flour to form a dough, and bake immediately.

Fried Bread.

Time, ten minutes.—Beat four eggs very light, add three tablespoonfuls of brown sugar, a little grated nutmeg, a tablespoonful of orange or rose water, and a quart of milk. Cut into slices, an inch thick, a stale loaf of bread; remove the crust from the sides, and cut each slice into halves. Butter your frying-pan, and when hot lay in your bread (dipped in the custard) and brown on both sides. Lay them on a hot dish, and sprinkle over them a little sugar.

Graham Bread.

Take two cups buttermilk or sour milk, one-half cup of best sugar-house syrup, one teaspoonful of soda, half teaspoonful of salt. Stir with a spoon to a stiff mass (not too stiff, or the bread will be too hard); put it into a three-pint or a two-quart basin, well buttered; put into a steamer over cold water, which gives the loaf more time for rising. Steam about an hour; then place it in the oven just long enough to give it a good rich brown color. Most excellent gems are made with sour milk and soda, with shortening and a little salt, stirred to a soft batter with Graham flour, and baked in a quick oven in gem irons or patty pans.

Frizzled Dried Beef.

Time, fifteen minutes; six persons.—Half-pound chipped beef, two tablespoonfuls of butter, half-pint of milk, two tablespoonfuls of flour, and dash of pepper. Chipped beef is perhaps one dish that is at least commonly prepared well. If the meat is very salt, scald it once or twice and then press it perfectly dry. Put the butter in a saute or frying-pan; stir or toss the beef in the butter until thoroughly hot; then sprinkle over the flour, mix carefully and add hastily the milk; bring to boiling point and stand over hot water.

Kidney Stew.

Time, thirty minutes; six persons.—Six veal kidneys, two tablespoonfuls of flour, half-pint of boiling water, one teaspoonful of Worcestershire sauce, one teaspoonful of tomato catsup, one teaspoonful of salt, two tablespoonfuls of butter. Wash and split the kidneys in halves. Remove the white tubes. Wash the kidneys, cover them with cold water, bring to boiling point, drain; cover with fresh boiling water, drain again. Be careful

10

that each time they are just brought to the boiling point, do not actually boil. Rub the butter and flour together; add it to the butter and flour; stir until boiling; add the Worcestershire sauce, tomato catsup and salt; bring again to a boil; add the kidneys; cover and stand over hot water for fifteen minutes. Calf's liver may be prepared in precisely the same way.

Kidneys Cooked in Their Fat.

Take three fresh sheep's kidneys, without removing their fat, cut into rounds about half an inch in thickness. Dip them in cream and season, then dip them into flour, and fry in bacon fat a golden brown on each side. Serve very hot on rounds of toast or fried bread.

Milk Toast.

One quart milk; when it comes to a boil thicken with one teaspoonful corn-starch; add salt. Toast the bread a light brown; butter each slice, put layers of toast in a covered dish and pour on the thickened milk, then more toast and milk, and so on till the dish is full; cover, let stand five minutes, and serve.

German Toast.

Prepare the tomatoes as for sauce, and while they are cooking toast some slices of bread very brown, but not burned; butter them both sides and pour the tomato sauce over them.

Corn Bread.

Time, one hour and a half.—Take one quart of sweet milk, corn meal enough to thicken, three eggs, half a cup of butter, two tablespoonfuls of brown sugar, one teaspoonful of soda, and two of cream of tartar; bake in a moderate oven.

Brown Bread.

Time, four to five hours.—One quart of Indian meal and one quart of rye, mixed well together; half a cup of molasses, one tablespoonful of salt, tablespoonful of cream of tartar, two-thirds of a tablespoonful of soda, dissolved in a pint of cold water. When dissolved wet the mixture with it, and if it does not thoroughly wet in add a little more. It should be nearly as stiff as bread.

How to Make Bread.

Bread making is an accomplishment of which every woman should be proud. It need never be a hard task, unless the woman makes hard work of it. Especially where the gas range is used, in which the heat is under absolute control, the very best and most satisfactory results can be attained. If the housekeeped has been in the habit of setting a sponge at night and insists upon that procedure, owing to a longer period of fermentation, a less quantity of yeast should be used than if set in the morning. Dry or compressed yeast may be used, but the compressed is preferable to dry when making bread during the day, as fermentation proceeds more rapidly. Certain proportions and conditions are necessary to obtain successful results. The better plan is to measure liquids as to the base of proportions, as flours vary in quality: One pint milk, one pint boiling water, two teaspoonfuls salt, one tablespoonful sugar, one tablespoonful butter, one yeast cake in one-quarter cup water. Put salt, sugar and shortening in mixing bowl, add milk and pour into it the boiling water. Dissolve yeast in one-quarter cup cold water. When liquid in bowl is lukewarm, add the dissolved yeast and flour enough to make a batter; beat well until full of bubbles, cover closely and keep warm for one hour, then add flour and knead into a smooth, velvety dough that will not stick to the hands. Place in warm place, allow to stand until it doubles in bulk and knead down, mold and put into pans. Allow to double in bulk again and bake in hot oven. Turn on both burners to heat the oven; let burn full on about eight to ten minutes. Turn off back burner and put in bread. The smaller loaves baked in the brick shaped pans can be baked in numbers to fill the oven to fullest capacity, changing from one side to the other, if necessary to insure even browning. According to thickness of loaves, thirty to sixty minutes should be allowed. Rolls may be lighter than bread and baked in hotter ovens.

Eggs a-la-Mode.

Remove the skin from a dozen tomatoes, medium size, cut them up in a saucepan, add a little butter, pepper and salt; when sufficiently boiled, beat up five or six eggs, and just before you serve turn them into the saucepan with the tomato, and stir them one way for two minutes, allowing them time to be well done.

Buckwheat Cakes.

Let the buckwheat be of the hulled sort, and fresh. Put into a two-quart pitcher one and one-half pints of tepid water; add four tablespoonfuls of bakers' or as much "compressed" yeast as will make one loaf of bread—other kinds in proportion—with a little salt. Then stir in buckwheat enough to make a thick batter; cover the pitcher and set away to rise over night, after beating thoroughly. In the morning add three tablespoonfuls of molasses and a quarter of a teaspoonful of soda, dissolved in about three tablespoonfuls of milk. Beat all well together, and pour the cakes from the pitcher upon a well-heated griddle.

Hominy Muffins.

Time, fifteen minutes.—Take two cups of fine hominy, boiled and cold; beat it smooth; stir in three cups of sour milk, half a cup of melted butter, two teaspoonfuls of salt, and two table-spoonfuls of white sugar; then add three eggs well beaten, one tablespoonful of soda dissolved in hot water, and one large cup of flour; bake quickly.

Flour Muffins.

Time, fifteen minutes.—One-half cup of butter, one-half cup of sugar, two cups of milk, three teaspoonfuls of yeast powder rubbed thoroughly into a scant quart of flour, and a little salt; bake in muffin rings.

Brown Flour Muffins.

Time, half an hour.—One quart tepid water, half cup yeast, one tablespoonful of Indian meal, two of molasses, two pints graham flour, one pint wheat, one teaspoonful of soda about half an hour before baking—as thick as soft gingerbread; bake half an hour—or in greased rings on a griddle.

Rice Muffins.

Time, fifteen minutes.—Take one cup of cold boiled rice, one pint of flour, two eggs, one quart of milk, one tablespoonful of butter, and one teaspoonful of salt; beat very hard and bake quickly.

Corn Muffins.

Time, fifteen minutes.—Two cups yellow Indian meal, one cup flour, three eggs, four tablespoonfuls of sugar, and a little salt, a piece of lard or butter the size of an egg, one teaspoonful saleratus and two of cream tartar (the cream tartar must be put in dry with the flour, and the saleratus mixed with a little warm water and put in last of all); mix all together with milk as thick as pound cake batter. Pour in corn-muffin-pans and bake in a hot oven.

13

Rusk.

One teacupful of butter, one cup of sugar, one egg, one bowl of milk or water, one-third cup of yeast. Mix stiff with a sponge over night, make out on pans in the morning; raise the second time.

Bread Crackers.

Take one pound of bread dough after it has risen; add two ounces of butter or lard; work well in dough; let rise again; roll out very thin; cut in cakes and bake till dry.

Breakfast Rolls.

Mix half an ounce of sifted white sugar in two pounds of the finest flour; make a hole in the center, and put in about two tablespoonfuls of fresh yeast, mixed with a little water; let it stand all night; in the morning add the yolks of two eggs, a piece of butter the size of a walnut, and sufficient warm milk to make it of a right consistency; divide into rolls (about twelve or fourteen); bake half an hour in a brisk oven.

French Rolls.

One pint of milk, one small cup of home-made yeast (you can try the baker's), flour enough to make a stiff batter; raise over night. In the morning add one egg, one tablespoonful of butter, and flour enough to make it fine and white), roll out, cut with a round tin and fold over; put them in a pan and cover very close. Set them in a warm place until they are very light; bake quickly.

Pan Doodles.

Make a sponge just as you do for bread over night. In the morning take from the bread-dough small pieces about the size of a walnut, shape them rather long than round; fry in boiling hot lard a light brown; serve hot in a covered dish; pull them open and butter them. You will find them both simple and delicious for breakfast.

Oatmeal Cakes.

Take two cups of cold boiled oatmeal; mix one egg through it; one tablespoonful of sugar, and prepared flour enough to make into cakes; dip each side into rolled cracker and fry brown.

Breakfast Pie.

Time, two hours.—A delicious pie. Make a standing crust; then a mixture of six eggs, a quart of milk, some finely powdered sweet herbs, a teaspoonful of white pepper; then line a pie dish with the crust; slice some ham very fine. Put a layer of ham, then part of your custard, and so on till the dish is full. Bake about two hours. When cold lift it out of the pie dish.

Batter Bread.

Take half a cup of bread crumbs soaked in a pint of milk and two eggs; beat this to a smooth batter; add two cups of Indian meal, one teaspoonful of salt, and one tablespoonful of butter; stir all together very hard, and bake in shallow tins very quickly.

Rice Cakes.

Take one cup of cold boiled rice, one pint of flour, one teaspoonful of salt, two eggs beaten lightly and milk enough to make this a thick batter; beat all together well and bake on a griddle.

Tea Biscuit.

One quart of sifted flour, a little salt, three teaspoonfuls of baking powder, a small handful of sugar; mix lightly through the flour; rub a large teaspoonful of lard through the dry mixture; mix with sweet milk or water, the colder the better; roll out soft to thickness of about one-third of an inch; cut with a large-sized cutter and bake in a really hot oven.

Dainty Muffins.

One-quarter cup butter, one-quarter cup sugar, one egg, about half a cup of milk, one and one-half cups pastry flour, three scant teaspoonfuls baking powder. Cream butter in cup, add sugar and cream together. Put in bowl, and add well beaten egg; sift baking powder with flour, and add, alternating with milk. Bake in hot buttered gem pans in moderately hot oven for twenty-five minutes.

Waffles.

Two cups flour, two level teaspoonfuls baking powder, one and one-third cups milk, one scant teaspoonful sugar, three eggs, two tablespoonfuls melted butter, one-half teaspoonful salt. Mix flour, baking powder, sugar and salt. Mix yolks, beaten well with milk; add to the flour gradually, beating in smoothly. Lastly fold in beaten whites. Have iron very clean, hot and well greased. Put enough batter in each side to fill not quite two-thirds full. Cover, cook waffles a minute longer on other side. Serve hot on hot plates.

Fritter Batter.

This is batter for the Swedish timbale cases made with timbale irons. Sift together one cup of pastry flour and one-half teaspoon of salt. Beat the yolks of four eggs light and add half a cup of milk or water. Then stir the liquid into the flour gradually, making a smooth batter, and add one tablespoon of olive oil or melted butter. Use the dover beater to whip the whites of eggs to a stiff froth and then add to the mixture and set away in a cool place for two hours or more. Have ready a kettle of hot fat, put iron into fat to heat. When hot, dip carefully into batter to cover about three-fourths of the mold, raise and immerse in fat. When lightly browned, take from fat, drain, tap handle quickly so as to detach the cooked case. Examine the first case. If thin or too thick, add flour or water to make of right consistency. Cases may be used at once, or set aside, rewarmed and filled at last moment before serving. Any creamed mixture of chicken, fish or vegetables may be used for filling.

The one who plays one of the most important parts in your little world is the COOK.

A world without cooks! just imagine.

How fortunate to have a little cook of your own who can supply wonderful dishes "Like Mother used to Make"—she is a wonder.

As an illustration, take a celebrated chef, the majority of them are married, and while they prepare the most elaborate dishes for others, they prefer home cooking, prepared by the little wife. Though he would gladly give lessons to the new wife, he'd rather have a piece of bread and butter from her hands than the finest meal he could prepare.

Would the idea of your husband knowing more about cooking than you did please you?

What a nice compliment to hear the remark: "My wife is a mighty fine cook, I can tell you; she beats her teacher." It makes a woman happy, for where is the woman who doesn't love being appreciated.

FISH.

Let great care be taken to well clean the fish before it is dressed. Fresh-water fish have often a muddy taste and smell, which may be got rid of by soaking them in strong salt and water before they are cooked.

Salt fish should be soaked in water before boiling, according to the time it has been in salt. When it is hard and dry, it will require thirty-six hours' soaking before it is dressed, and the water must be changed three or four times. When fish is not very salt, twenty-four hours, or even one night, will suffice.

To Fry Fish.

Cleanse them thoroughly, dry them on a folded cloth, dredge flour lightly over them, brush them with a well-beaten egg, then dip them in fine breadcrumbs.

Have ready enough fine oil, or melted lard or beef dripping (clarified), to entirely cover the fish. Place the frping-pan over a clear fire. Let the lard reach the boiling point, and then immerse the fish in it. You may try whether the fat is hot enough by letting a drop of cold water fall into it from the end of your spoon. If the hot fat spits, it is ready for use. Then fry, turning the fish when one side is browned to the other. When it is done, serve it extremely dry on a white cloth or embossed fish paper.

To Broil Fish.

A clear fire is required. Rub the bars of your gridiron with dripping or a piece of beef suet, to prevent the fish from sticking to it. Put a good piece of butter into a dish, work into it enough salt and pepper to season the fish. Lay the fish on it when it is broiled, and with a knife blade put the butter over every part. Serve very hot.

To Boil Fish.

Put the fish in the saucepan, and a little more than half cover it with boiling water. Cover the lid closely and boil gently until done. To determine when a fish is sufficiently boiled, draw it up upon the fish plate, and if the thickest part of the fish can be easily divided from the bone with a knife, it should be at once taken from the water. A little saltpetre or a few spoonfuls of vinegar may be added to the water to render the boiled fish firm. Some cooks prefer to steep the fish in salt and water from five to ten minutes before putting it in the kettle to cook, instead of putting salt in the water in which it is to boil. By this this means less scum rises.

18

Codfish Balls.

Have the ingredients cooked on the day you wish them to be eaten. Put your codfish to soak a day and a half, and then boil until tender. Have your potatoes boiling, too. When the fish is done, pull every lump, no matter how small, apart, until it is light and feathery. Mash the potatoes until they are perfectly smooth; add a little cream or milk, and a little butter, but not enough to color them; mix all thoroughly; roll into fat, smooth balls, about one-half inch thick. Be careful to make them a good shape. A little raw onion, chopped fine, is delicious mixed through them, just sufficient to flavor. Fry a good brown, in plenty of hot lard. Cooked oysters, laid on before eating, make them still better.

Baked Fish.

Select fresh, firm-fleshed fish for baking, clean thoroughly, cut off fins, leaving head and tail, wipe dry and pin oiled paper on the tail. Dust the inside with salt. Have needle with thread ready for sewing up fish as it is stuffed. Cut strips of fat bacon or salt pork to lay in gashes or over top of fish, to baste in baking. Fill with

Stuffing for Baked Fish.

Put in a bowl one cup of bread crumbs from loaf two or three days old; add one-quarter teaspoonful salt, one-eighth teaspoon pepper, one teaspoon onion juice, one teaspoon minced parsley, two level teaspoons finely chopped sweet midget cucumber pickles (one teaspoon of capers if you have them and are liked), one-quarter cup melted butter. If crumbs are not too dry, no moisture need be added. The stuffing if slightly "crumbly" is more delicate. Put in lightly, sew up fish and form a horseshoe or letter S shape. On each side cut gashes to make body of fish turn in shape, and fill them with the pork strips. Skewer and tie in shape; put strips of pork in bottom of pan, rest fish on these and add one cup hot water to pan. Baste with hot water, to which a little salt has been added. Have the oven hot, for fish must begin baking at once. Within five minutes or less, a hissing sound should be heard. Upon this first heat of the oven will depend the success of the baking. The fish will be delicious, juicy and tender if baked just right, and those who have not liked fish at all will relish a fish baked in this manner. Allow twenty-five to thirty minutes for baking a fish of three or four pounds. When done, place on platter, remove paper, skewers, threads, pork strips, and garnish with saratoga potatoes, lemon points and parsley or water cress. Serve with Hollandaise sauce.

Baked Slice of Halibut.

Time, thirty minutes; six persons.—One thick slice of halibut, one level teaspoonful of salt, parsley, one small onion, one salt spoonful of pepper, one tablespoonful of butter, one-half cup of water, one lemon; melt the butter; chop the onion, put in the bottom of the baking pan, put on top of the halibut steak, dust with salt and pepper, and then the melted butter. Bake in a quick oven, or, if you have a gas stove, in the broiling chamber, for thirty minutes, basting once or twice. The steak must be nicely browned. Dish, strain over any sauce that may be left over in the pan, garnish with parsley and lemon, and send at once to the table.

Lobster a-la-Bordelaise.

Time, forty-five minutes; six persons.—One good sized lobster, two ounces of butter, one bay leaf, one salt spoonful of pepper, one-half pound of fresh mushrooms or one can of mushrooms, one pint of boiling water, one small onion, one salt spoonful of celery seed, one level teaspoonful of salt. Put the butter and onion, chopped, into a saucepan, cook until the onion is slightly browned, then add the flour, when boiling add all the seasonings. Simmer gently for ten minutes, strain, add the mushrooms; simmer ten minutes longer and stand the sauce over hot water while you cut the lobster into good sized pieces, put the lobster into the sauce, cover the pan closely and stand it over hot water for ten minutes and it is ready to serve. This may be served on toast in pate shells, or in a vol-au-vent.

Fish Cakes.

One pint bowl salt codfish, picked very fine, two pint bowls of whole, raw, peeled potatoes; put together in cold water and boil until the potatoes are thoroughly cooked; remove from fire and drain off all the water; mash with potato-masher; add piece of butter the size of an egg, two well-beaten eggs, and a little pepper; mix well with a wooden spoon; have a frying-pan with boiling lard or drippings, into which drop a spoonful of mixture and fry brown; do not freshen the fish before boiling with potatoes, and do not mold cakes, but drop from spoon.

20

Trout a l'Espagnol.

Scale the trout and clean it by the gills; put inside it butter mixed with parsley, chopped onions, pepper, and salt; then dress the fish with oil, parsley, onions, thyme, laurel, salt, and pepper, and place it on a griddle, wrapped in oil-paper, dressing and all. When cooked, take the paper and herbs off, and cover with anchovy sauce.

Fish Fritters.

Take salt codfish and soak it over night. In the morning throw the water off the fish, put on fresh, and set it on the range until it comes to a boil. Do not let it boil, as that will harden it. Then pick it up very fine, season with pepper, mace, and perhaps a little salt. Make a batter of a pint of milk and three eggs, stir in the fish, and fry in small cakes. Any kind of codfish makes nice fritters.

Turbot a-la-Creme.

Time, one hour.—Take five pounds of halibut or cod; boil thoroughly in salt and water; when done, drain it, and when cool flake it, taking out all the bones. One quart of cream set in a saucepan of hot water, some sprigs of parsley, two tablespoonfuls of corn-starch; cook it until it is flavored, then strain out the parsley and half a pound of butter to the cream; take the dish you serve it in and put first a layer of fish, then a layer of cream, a sprinkle of cayenne pepper, then a layer of cracker crumbs, and so on until the dish is full; put the last layer of cracker crumbs; bake it an hour at least; garnish with parsley.

Fresh Halibut Fish-balls.

To two pounds of boiled halibut add double the quantity of hot mashed potatoes; the fish must be picked in small pieces; add butter the size of an egg, a teaspoonful of powdered sugar, salt, and two eggs; mix them well, make them into round, flat balls, and when the weather is cold they can stand over night, but in summer they must be made in the morning. Have a kettle of boiling hot lard, put in only a few at a time, and boil them until they are a nice light brown. If the lard is not quite boiling they will soak the fat, and if too hot they will come out black instead of brown. If the fish, potatoes, etc.. seem too dry when you mix it, add a very little milk.

Salmagundi.

Take the bones out of one dozen salt herring or shad and cut the flesh fine; wash two or three times in cold water; squeeze the water well out; slice eight onions thin; put fish and onions together and put on cold vinegar and pepper.

Halibut Steaks.

Wash and wipe the steaks dry; beat up two or three eggs and roll out some hard crackers very fine; salt each steak and then dip into the beaten eggs, and after into the cracker crumbs, and fry in hot fat.

To Cook Shad-roes.

First partially boil them in a small covered pan and then fry in hot lard, after covering or sprinkling with flour. The slices may also be simply dried in a cloth, floured and broiled over a clear fire; but they require the greatest care then to prevent them from burning. The gridiron is always rubbed with suet first.

Boiled Salmon.

Salmon is put into warm water instead of cold, in order to preserve its color and set the curd. It should be thoroughly well dressed to be wholesome. Scale it, empty and wash it with the greatest care. Do not leave any blood in the inside that you can remove. Boil the salt rapidly in the fish-kettle for a minute or two, taking off the scum as it rises; put in the salmon, first trussing it in the shape of the letter S, and let it boil gently until it is thoroughly done. Take it from the water on the fish-plate, let it drain, put it on a hot folded fish napkin, and garnish with slices of lemon. Sauce: Shrimp or lobster. Send up dressed cucumber with salmon.

Broiled Salmon.

Time, ten to fifteen minutes.—Cut slices of an inch or an inch and a half thick from the middle of a large salmon; dust a little cayenne pepper over them; wrap them in oiled or buttered paper, and broil them over a clear fire, first rubbing the bars of the gridiron with suet.

Cod's Head and Shoulder.

Time, half an hour or more.—Cod's head and shoulders; four ounces of salt to each gallon of water; a little horseradish. Rub a little salt down the bone and the thick part of the fish, and tie a fold or two of wide tape round it to prevent its breaking. Lay it in a fish-kettle with sufficient cold water to cover it, with salt in the above proportion; add three spoonfuls of vinegar and a little horseradish. Let the water be brought just to the verge of boiling; then draw the fish-kettle to the side of the fire, to simmer gently till the fish is done, which can be ascertained by trying it with a fish slice to see if the meat can be separated easily from the bone; skim it well and carefully. When done, drain it and slip it off the fish strainer on a napkin neatly folded in a dish. Garnish with double parsley, lemon and the roe and liver of the cod. If the cod be crimped, it will re-puire a shorter time to dress it.

Picked Cod.

Time, fifteen minutes.—About one pound and a half of dressed cod; a little oyster and egg sauce; two hard-boiled eggs, and four parsnips, or some mashed potatoes. Pick about a pound and a half of dressed codfish into flakes, and put it in layers, with a little oyster and egg sauce alternately, in a stewpan. Make it thoroughly hot. When it is done, pile it in the center of the dish, and serve with mashed potatoes in a wall round it, browned with a salamander, or garnish it with slices of hard-boiled eggs and parsnips cut into shapes.

Salt Cod.

Time, one hour.—Put the cod in water the night before it is wanted, and let it soak all night; boil it; lay it in a dish, and send it up hot, with egg sauce. If it be preferred, instead of the egg sauce, boil parsnips quite tender, mash them with butter, cream or milk, and spread them round the salt fish.

Baked Eels.

Time, three-quarters of an hour.—Skin, empty, and thorough-ly wash four large eels, cut off the heads, and divide them into rather short pieces, wipe them very dry, dip each piece into a seasoning of cayenne, salt, minced parsley, and a little powdered savory herbs, put them into a deep dish, cover them with veal stock, put a thick paper or cover over the dish, and set it in the oven until the eels are tender. Skim off the fat, take the pieces of fish carefully out on a hot dish to keep warm, and stir into the gravy the wine, strained lemon juice and sauce; make it just boil up, and pour it over the fish. Garnish with sliced lemon.

Fried Eels.

Time, eighteen or twenty minutes.—Prepare and wash the eels, wipe them thoroughly dry, and dredge over them a very little flour; if large, cut them into pieces of about four inches long, brush them over with egg, dip them in bread crumbs, and fry them in hot fat. If small they should be curled round and fried, first dipped into egg and bread crumbs. Serve them up garnished with fried parsley.

Yacht Oyster Stew.

Time, half an hour.—Strain, cook and skim the juice of twenty-four oysters; boil celery and a quarter of a small onion in a little water for half an hour or until the celery is well cooked; then add a pint of milk or cream, a tablespoonful of butter, a tablespoonful of pounded crackers, a teaspoonful of Worcestershire sauce, salt, pepper, the oysters, and cooked juice, and boil all three minutes, or until the edges of the oysters shrivel.

To Stew Oysters.

Time, ten minutes.—After pouring off the juice, put the oysters in some salt water and pass each one between the thumb and finger to get rid of the slime. Then to 100 oysters add half a pound of butter rubbed up with a teaspoonful of flour; stir for ten minltes or till done, then add a half pint of cream, but do not permit it to boil, otherwise the cream will curdle; add salt and cayenne to the taste.

Scalloped Oysters.

Time, a quarter of an hour.—Butter some tin scallop shells, or if you have not any, a small tart dish. Strew in a layer of grated bread, then put some thin slices of butter, then oysters enough to fill your shells or dish. Cover them thickly with bread crumbs, again add slices of butter. Pepper the whole well, add a little of the liquor kept from the oysters. Put butter over the whole surface, and bake in a quick oven. Serve them in their shells or in the dish. Brown them with a salamander. If you have not one, make the kitchen shovel redhot and hold it over closely enough to brown your scallops.

Oyster Patties.

Cover some small tins, called patty-pans, with puff paste; cut it round, and put in the center a small piece of bread (to prevent the top and bottom from collapsing); cover it with paste, slightly pinch the edges together, and bake in a brisk oven a quarter of an hour. Then, having bearded and parboiled a dozen large oysters, cut them in quarters, and put them in a stewpan with an ounce of butter, a teaspoonful of flour, mixed with their liquor, and the broth from the beards(which you must stey in a small saucepan, with a little stock gravy and two or three shreds of lemon). Season with a very little salt, a quarter of a teaspoonful of powdered mace, and the same quantity of cayenne; then gradually add three tablespoonfuls of cream. Mix well; then with a thin knife open the patties, take out the bread, put in a spoonful of the oysters and cream gravy; put the covers on again and serve hot.

Pickled Oysters.

Scald, beard, and wash large, fat oysters in their own liquor; strain it, and to every pint put a glass of white wine, mace, nutmeg, a good many white peppercorns, and a little salt, if necessary; simmer the oysters for four or five minutes; put vinegar, in the proportion of a glass to the pint, to the liquor, and boil it up; skim this pickle and pour it over the oysters, and when cold cork and close them up tight.

Soft-Shell Crabs.

Soft-shell crabs must be dipped in beaten egg, and then in grated bread or cracker crumbs, and thrown into a hot frying-pan, in which salt pork has been friend out for the purpose; it gives them a much better flavor than butter or lard.

Oyster Fritters.

Time, five or six minutes.—Beard some good-sized oysters, make a thick omelet batter with four eggs and a tablespoonful of milk, dip each oyster into the batter, and then into grated bread, fry them a nice color, and use them to garnish fried fish.

Scallops.

Time, half an hour.—Cover the scallops with beaten egg and bread-crumbs, well seasoned with pepper, salt and minced parsley, and fry them nicely. Put them to keep hot, dredge flour into the frying-pan to take up the grease, mix in water enough for gravy, season with pepper and salt, thicken it if required, make the scallops hot in it, and serve them with the gravy together. Lemon pickle may be added.

They may also be floured and fried, and then stewed.

25

To Stew Mussels.

Time, ten minutes.—Clean the shells thoroughly with repeated washings, and cook them until they open, as mentioned above. Pick them out of the shells, and as you do so save the liquor that runs from them, and pick out from each one the little hairy appendage to be found at the root of the little member shaped like a tongue. To the mussels, thus prepared, put half a pint of the liquor saved, and if there is not enough of it eke out the quantity with a little of the liquor in which they were boiled, poured off clear. Put in a blade of mace, thicken it with a piece of butter rolled in flour, let them stew gently for a few minutes, and serve them on toast.

To Boil Herrings.

Time, twenty minutes.—Clean and wash the fish; dry them in a cloth, and rub over them a little vinegar and salt. Skewer them with their tails in their mouths, lay them on a strainer in a stewpan, and when the water boils put them in, and let them continue simmering slowly for about twenty minutes. When they are done, drain and place them in the dish with the heads turned in to the center; garnish with scraped horseradish, and serve with parsley and butter sauce.

To Bake Herrings.

Time, one hour.—Clean and wash two herrings, lay them on a dish or board, and rub well over and into them a spoonful of pepper, one of salt, and twelve cloves pounded. Lay them in an earthen pan, cover them with vinegar, add two or three bay leaves, and tie them over with a thick paper. Put them into a moderate oven, and bake them for an hour. To be eaten cold.

Fried Herrings.

Time, six or eight minutes.—Clean and scale the fish, and dry them thoroughly in a cloth. When they are quite dry, fry them to a bright color. The herring, being so rich a fish, should be fried with less butter than fish of most kinds, and well drained, and dried afterwards. A nice sauce to eat with herrings is sugar, mustard, and a little salt and vinegar. Some serve melted butter, but herrings, are too rich to eat with a rich sauce. Crisp parsley may be used as a garnish.

To Dress Lobsters.

When sent to table, separate the body from the tail, remove the large claws, and crack them at each joint carefully, and split the tail down the middle with a sharp knife; place the

26

body upright in the center of a dish on a napkin, and arrange the tail and claws on each side. Garnish it with double parsley.

To Dress Boiled Crabs.

Empty the large shell; mix the flesh with a very little oil, vinegar, salt, white pepper, and cayenne to your taste, replace the meat in the large shell, and place it in the dish with the claws.

To Pickle Fish.

Take any freshly caught fish, clean and scale them, wash and wipe them dry. Cut them into slices a few inches thick, put them in a jar with some salt, some allspice, and a little horse-radish. When filled, cover them with good strong vinegar. Cover it well with a good cover. Let it stand in your oven a few hours. Don't let the oven be too hot. This will keep six months. Put it immediately in the cellar, and in a few days they will be fit for use.

Clam Chowder.

Twenty-five clams, chopped fine; six potatoes, chopped fine; two onions, chopped fine; a piece of salt pork, also chopped, and butter about the size of an egg; salt and pepper to taste the clam juice and one pint of milk and the same of water; six crackers rolled, one nutmeg, teaspoonful celery seed. Boil these slowly for at least four hours, adding water if it becomes too thick; half an hour before serving add coffee cupful of tomato catsup and two tablespoonfuls of Worcestershire sauce. When ready for table add tumbler of sherry; cut a lemon in slices and serve with it.

Fried Oysters.

Select fine, large oysters, dry them out of their own liquor. Have ready a plate of eggs and a plate of bred crumbs. Let them lay in the egg a few minutes, and then roll them in the bread crumbs, allowing them to remain in these for a minute or two; this will make them adhere, and not come off as a skin when in the pan. Fry in half butter and half lard, in order to give them a rich brown. Make it very hot before putting the oysters in.

Clam Fritters.

Take twelve large or twenty-five small claims from their shells; if the clams are large, divide them. Mix two gills of wheat flour with one gill of milk, half as much of the clam liquor, and one egg well beaten. Make the batter smooth, and then stir in the clams. Drop the batter by tablespoonfuls in boiling lard; let them fry gently, turning them when done on one side.

27

SOUPS.

It is of great importance that every one, and most especially those who labor hard, should take a little light soup at the be-.ginning of a dinner, it warms and stimulates the stomach and prepares it for the digestion of the heavier foods to follow.

Soup Garnishings.

Under this heading we place croutons of various sizes and shapes, which are perhaps the most active of soup garnishings; cooked vegetables cut into fancy shapes, tiny egg balls, force meat balls, marrow or suet balls, are also sightly and palatable.

Stock.

All meat soups have "stock" for their basis. Beef and veal make the best stock, but mutton, if previously broiled or roasted, is very good. The Digester or Stock-pot should be made the receptacle of all sorts of meat bones, either broken or crushed, as the large proportion of gelatinous matter they contain is the basis or jelly of the stock, to which it can be added at pleasure.

Winter (Split) Pea Soup.

Time, three hours.—Soak a quart of split peas in soft water for twelve or fourteen hours, and remove those which float on the top. Then simmer in two quarts of water until tender; put them in your stewpan; add two quarts of beef stock, about a couple of pounds of shin of beef, any odd meat bones, chopped up, and a slice of ham; a head of celery, six onions, three each of carrots and turnips—all peeled and sliced—and seasoning to taste . Simmer the whole for two or three hours, stirring and skimming from time to time; pass all through a fine hair sieve, give it one boil, and serve with toasted bread.

Pot-Au-Feu.

Time, three hours.—Take shin of beef or cold beefsteak or roast, or anything of that kind; put in grated carrot (because that gives a flavor and a nice color), turnips, potatoes, a little browned flour, and plenty of salt and pepper; add a little garlic, half an onion, and some parsley. Boil two or three hours; strain after all is cooked.

Soup Julienne.

Time, forty-five minutes; six persons.—One small turnip, half-cup of fresh green peas, one head of lettuce, one teaspoonful of salt, one and one-half quarts of boiling water, half cup of tender young beans, one potato, one salt spoonful of pepper.

Cut the carrot, turnip and potato in small strips; shell the peas and beans. Put the carrot and turnip in unsalted water and cook until tender, about thirty minutes. Put the beans in salted water, cook twenty minutes; add the peas, cook ten minutes and drain. Throw the potato in unsalted water and cook five minutes. Drain all the vegetables, mix and add four nice lettuce leaves cut into shreds; add the vegetables and seasons, bring to a boil and serve.

Potato Soup.

Time, two hours.—Eight potatoes, two turnips, four large onions, boiled together (in beef, mutton or poultry water) to a jam; then strained through a colander; then add butter rubbed in flour (a little), with cream or sweet milk, pepper and salt; chopped parsley in the bottom of the tureen; let soup boil well, then pour over the parsley.

Mock Bisque Soup.

Stew a can of tomatoes, and strain. Add a pinch of baking soda, to remove the acidity. In another saucepan boil three pints of milk; thicken with a tablespoonful of corn-starch previously mixed with a little cold milk; add lump of butter size of an egg; salt and pepper to taste; mix with tomatoes; let all come once to the boil and serve.

Clam Soup.

Time, one hour.—Twenty-five clams, opened, raw and chopped fine; add three quarts of water; boil them one-half hour, then add a pint of milk, one onion chopped fine, thicken with butter and flour; beat three eggs in the tureen and pour your broth over them boiling hot.

Black Bean Soup.

Time, five hours.—Take a large knuckle of veal, add to it four quarts of water and one quart of black beans that have been soaked in water over night, and let them boil with the veal four or five hours; also, a small bit of onion and a dozen whole cloves, some salt and pepper; cut three hard-boiled eggs and two lemons into slices and put into the bottom of your tureen, and strain the soup, boiling hot, upon them. If the water boils away, you must keep adding to it, as this recipe ought to make a gallon of soup. It should be of the consistency of pea soup. If you have no veal, the bones of salt pork make a good substitute, but not equal to the knuckle.

Mock Turtle Soup.

Time, twelve hours.—Take about ten pounds of shin beef, cut it into small pieces, and fry the lean parts a light brown; put the rest of the beef (i. e., the fat part) into a stewpan with boiling water, and stew it for eight hours, with a bunch of sweet herbs and two onions; when cold take off the fat. Then get half a calf's head with the skin on, half boil it, and cut it into small square pieces and put them with the lean beef and the soup into the same pot, and let them stew altogether until quite tender. Thicken it with a very little flour; add a little pounded mace and cloves, and a grate of nutmeg, two spoonfuls of mushroom catsup, and pepper and salt to taste. A wine glass of sherry or white wine improves it. It should be served with egg balls and lemon.

Tomato Soup.

Time, one hour and a quarter.—Take twelve large tomatoes, peel and chop them; boil ripe ones an hour, then stir in a half a teaspoonful of soda; when the foaming ceases add two soft crackers rolled very fine; add a quart of milk, one tablespoonful of butter and boil fifteen minutes. Salt and pepper to taste. If too thick, add a little boiling water or milk.

Oyster Soup.

Time, half an hour.—To one hundred oysters take one quart of milk, half a pint of water, four spoonfuls of flour, half a cup of butter, and one teaspoonful of salt, with a very little cayenne pepper. Boil and skim the liquor off the oysters. Steam the flour and butter over the tea-kettle until soft enough to beat to a froth; then stir it in the liquor while boiling; after which add the other ingredients, and throw in the oysters, allowing them merely to scald.

Green Pea Soup.

Time, two hours.—Take two quarts of green peas, one small onion and a sprig of parsley cut fine; add two quarts of hot water and boil slowly for half an hour, then add a pint of small new potatoes which have been peeled and laid in cold water an hour; put in a teaspoonful of sugar and a little salt; boil till the potatoes are done; now add a teacupful of cream or a pint of milk, boil a minute or two, and serve with small slices of toasted bread or gems cut in halves.

30

Chicken Soup.

Time, four hours.—Boil a pair of chickens with great care, skimming constantly, and keeping them covered with water. When tender, take out the chicken and remove every bone from the meat; put a large lump of butter into a frying-pan and dredge the chicken meat well with flour, lay in the hot pan; fry a nice brown and keep it hot and dry. Take a pint of the chicken water and stir in two large spoonfuls of curry powder, two of butter and one of flour, one teaspoonful of salt and a little cayenne; stir until smooth, then mix it with the broth in the pot; when well mixed, simmer five minutes, then add the browned chicken. Serve with rice.

Macaroni Soup.

Time, three-quarters of an hour.—The macaroni must be boiled in water for ten minutes, strained and put into boiling stock, in the proportion of half a pound to the gallon; simmer slowly for half an hour, and serve very hot, with grated cheese on a separate dish.

Kidney Soup.

Time, six hours.—Add to the liquor from a boiled leg of mutton a bullock's kidney, put it over the fire and when half done take out the kidney and cut it into pieces the size of dice. Add three sticks of celery, three or four turnips, and the same of carrots, all cut small, and a bunch of sweet herbs, tied together. Season to your taste with pepper and salt. Let it boil slowly for five or six hours, adding the catsup. When done take out the herbs, and serve the vegetables in the soup. It is always better (as all soups are) made the day before it is wanted.

Scotch Barley Broth.

Time, two hours.—Take six pounds of the thick flank of beef, and cover it with six quarts of water, and a quarter of a pound of barley; boil it gently for an hour, skimming it frequently. Then add three heads of celery, two carrots, two turnips cut into pieces, one onion, a bunch of sweet herbs, and a little parsley; boil all together till you find the broth very good. Season it with salt. Then take out the beef, the onion, and sweet herbs; pour the broth into the tureen and put the beef in a dish garnished with carrots and turnips.

31

Ox-Tail Soup.

Time, four hours and a half.—Cut up two ox-tails, separating them at the joints; put them into a stewpan with about an ounce and a half of butter, a head of celery, two onions, two turnips, and two carrots cut into slices, and a quarter of a pound of lean ham cut very thin; the pepper corns and savory herbs, and about a half pint of cold water. Stir it over a quick fire for a short time to extract the flavor of the herbs, or until the pan is covered with a glaze. Then pour in three quarts of water, skim it well, and simmer slowly for four hours, or until the tails are tender. Take them out, strain the soup, stir in a little flour to thicken it, add a glass of port wine, the catsup, and half a head of celery (previously boiled and cut into small pieces). Put the pieces of tail into the stewpan with the strained soup. Boil it up for a few minutes, and serve. This soup can be served clear, by omitting the flour and adding to it carrots and turnips cut into fancy shapes, with a head of celery in slices. These may be boiled in a little of the soup, and put into the tureen before sending it to table.

SAUCES.

An appetizing sauce covers "A Multitude of Sins." It is easily made even with little material and at short notice. A rounding teaspoonful of butter rubbed with a rounding table-spoonful of flour is sufficient thickening to each half pint of liquid.

For drawn butter plain water is used instead of milk, so by changing the seasonings and liquids a great variety of sauces are easily made. An ordinary stew, with a carefully made sauce, makes an attractive dish, left over vegetables, meats, etc., can be used to advantage for a beautiful sauce.

SAUCES AND GRAVIES.

The thickest saucepans should be used for this operation, and only wooden spoons should be used for stirring. Remember, also, that your saucepan must be exquisitely clean and fresh if you would have your cause a success, especially when it is melted butter. Let your fire be clear and not too fierce.

Receipt for Melting Butter.

Time, two or three minutes.—Put about two ounces or two ounces and a half of butter into a very clean saucepan, with two tablespoonfuls of water, dredge in a little flour, and shake it over a clear fire, one way, until it boils. Then pour it into your tureen and serve as directed.

Common Egg Sauce.

Time, twenty minutes.—Boil two eggs for twenty minutes, then take them out of the egg saucepan and put them in cold water to get cool, shell them and cut them into very small dice, put the minced eggs into a very hot sauce tureen, and pour over them a quarter of a pint of boiling melted butter. Stir the sauce round to mix the eggs with it.

Parsley Sauce.

Time, six or seven minutes.—Wash the parsley thoroughly, boil it for six or seven minutes till tender, then press the water well out of it; chop it very fine; make half or a quarter of a pint of melted butter as required (the less butter the less parsley, of course), mix it gradually with the hot melted butter.

Oyster Sauce.

Time, five minutes.—Stew the beards of one dozen oysters in their own juice with half a teacupful of good clear gravy; strain it off, add it to the melted butter—which should be ready—put in the oysters, and let them simmer gently for three minutes.

Anchovy Sauce (for Fish).

Time, four minutes.—Stir three dessert spoonfuls of anchovy essence into half a pint of good melted butter, add a seasoning to your taste, and boil it up for a minute or two. Use plenty of cayenne and a little mace in this sauce.

Glaze.

Boil some very strong clear gravy or jelly over a quick fire to the thickness of cream, stirring it constantly until it will adhere like jelly to the spoon. It must then be immediately poured out of the stewpan; the greatest care is required during the time of thickening to prevent it from burning. When required for use, dissolve it by placing the jar (or whatever it may be kept in) in boiling water, and brushing it over the meat two or three times, when it will form a clear varnish. Any kind of very rich stock can be boiled down to a glaze. To be used for hams, tongues, etc.

To Brown Flour.

Time, five minutes.—Put some flour in a pan or dish, and set it in the oven or over the fire. Stir it about that it may not burn; but let it brown well. Keep it in a dredging box for browning ordinary gravies.

A Cheap Brown Gravy.

Time, two hours.—Take a pound of gravy beef and a sheep's melt, cut it into slices, dredge them with flour, and fry them lightly in butter; then pour in hot quite a pint of water. Add a seasoning of pepper and salt, a small onion, and a piece of celery cut into slices. Set the stewpan over the fire, and let it stew slowly for two hours. Skim it well; strain it; add a spoonful of catsup, and set it by for use.

Gravy for Hashes, Etc.

Time, two hours and a quarter.—Break some bones, and put them into a stewpan, with any spare cuttings of meat you may have; add a little pepper, salt and twelve allspice, half a head of celery, and a bunch of sweet herbs, and simmer it for about two hours, with sufficient water to cover it. Cut a small onion into slices, fry it in a piece of butter, and boil it up with the gravy for fifteen or twenty minutes. Strain it into another stewpan, with two tablespoonfuls of walnut catsup and a piece of butter rolled in flour, boil it up and it will be ready for your meat.

White Gravy.

Time, four hours.—This gravy is the stock of several white sauces, and is made thus: Put into a quart stewpan three pounds of lean veal, cut into dice, and half a pound of lean ham, cut smaller; add a glass of cold water, and put over the fire until the "white glaze," or jelly, forms on the bottom of the pan:

then add three pints of cold water, a bunch of savory herbs, a sliced onion and a blade of mace. Let it slowly come to a boil, then add a little salt, skim carefully, and simmer slowly for about three hours; strain, and when quite cold, remove all the fat.

Gravy for a Goose or Ducks.

Time, three hours.—Put one set of giblets and half a pound of lean beef into a stewpan, with three sage leaves, one onion, some whole pepper, salt, and three pints of water, and boil it for three hours; then add a glass of port wine, with a spoonful of flour mixed smooth to thicken it, and boil it again for two or three minutes.

Bread Sauce for Roast Turkey or Game.

Time, one hour and a half.—Peel and slice an onion and simmer it in a pint of new milk until tender, break the bread into pieces and put it into a small stewpan. Strain the hot milk over it, cover it close, and let it soak for an hour. Then beat it up smooth with a fork, add the pounded mace, cayenne, salt, and an ounce of butter; boil it up, and serve it in a tureen. The onion must be taken out before the milk is poured over the bread.·

Apple Sauce.

Time, twenty minutes.—Pare, core and cut into slices eight good boiling apples; put them into a saucepan with sufficient water to moisten and prevent them from burning, boil them until sufficiently tender to pulp. Then beat them up smoothly with a piece of butter, and put sugar to your taste.

Horseradish Sauce, for Boiled Mutton or Roast Beef.

Time, two or three minutes.—Mix a stick of grated horse-radish with a wine glass of cream, a teaspoonful of mustard, and a pinch of salt, then stir in half a tumbler of the best vinegar, and a pinch of salt. Bruise them with a spoon, and when thoroughly mixed together, serve in a tureen.

Mint Sauce for Roast Lamb.

Two tablespoonfuls of chopped green mint; one tablespoonful of pounded sugar; and a quarter of a pint of vinegar. Pick and wash the green mint very clean, chop it fine, mix the sugar and vinegar in a sauce tureen, put in the mint, and let it stand.

Common Onion Sauce.

Time, nearly half an hour.—Peel four or six white onions and boil them till they are tender, press the water from them and chop them very fine. Make half a pint of milk hot, pulp the onions into it, add a little piece of butter, a salt spoonful of salt, and pepper to your taste.

Arrowroot Sauce for Plum Pudding.

Time, fifteen minutes.—Rub very smoothly a dessert spoonful of arrowroot in a little water, or in a glass of white wine, squeeze in the juice of half a lemon add the pounded sugar, and pour gradually in half a pint of water. Stir it very quickly over a clear fire until it boils. Serve it with plum pudding. This sauce may be flavored with anything you prefer.

White Wine Sauce.

Time, five minutes.—Add to half a pint of good melted butter, four spoonfuls of white wine, the grated rind of half a lemon, and the sugar pounded and sifted. Let it boil, and serve with plum, bread, or boiled batter pudding, etc.

Cranberry Sauce.

Time, twenty minutes.—Take a quart of cranberries, a pint of sugar and a pint of water. Boil slowly, and when the berries are soft, beat well and strain through a colander.

White Sauce.

In three tablespoonfuls of nice, melted butter mix thoroughly one table-spoonful of sifted flour, add three-fourths of a pint of milk, boil once, and then stir quickly. For color, add a little yolk of egg, and for flavor, lemon juice.

Tomato Sauce.

Time, one hour.—Remove the skin and seeds from about a dozen tomatoes, slice them and put them in a stewpan, with pepper and salt to taste, and three pounded crackers. Stew slowly one hour.

Horseradish.

Wash the horseradish very clean, and lay it in cold water for nearly an hour; then scrape it into very fine shreds with a sharp knife. Place some of it in a glass dish, and arrange the remainder as a garnish for roast beef, or many kinds of boiled fish.

FORCEMEATS OR STUFFING.

Sage and Onion Stuffing, for Geese, Ducks or Pork.

Wash, peel and boil three onions in two waters to extract the strong flavor, and scald eight sage leaves for a few minutes. Chop the onions and leaves very fine, mix them with five ounces of bread-crumbs, seasoned with pepper and salt, a piece of butter broken into pieces, and the yolk of one egg.

Oyster Forcemeat.

Take off the beards from a half pint of oysters, wash them well in their own liquor, and mince them very fine; mix with them the peel of half a lemon chopped small, a sprig of parsley, a seasoning of salt, nutmeg, and a very little cayenne, and about an ounce of butter in small pieces. Stir into these in-gredients five ounces of bread-crumbs, and when thoroughly mixed together, bind it with the yolk of an egg and part of the oyster liquor.

Egg Balls, for Made Dishes or Soup.

Time, twenty minutes to boil the eggs.—Poudn the hard-boiled yolks of eight eggs in a mortar until very smooth; then mix with them the yolks of four raw eggs, a little salt, and a dust or so of flour to make them bind. Roll them into small balls, boil them in water and then add them to any made dishes or soups for which they may be required.

Fried Parsley.

Time, two minutes.—Fried parsley is the cheapest and commonest of garnishings, but it requires to be very nicely done. Wash and pick the parsley, and dry it thoroughly in a cloth. Then put it in a wire basket, and hold it in boiling dripping for two minutes. Take it out of the basket and dry it well before the fire that it may become very crisp. The drip-ping in which it is fried should be quite boiling. If you have no wire basket, fry the parsley as quickly as possible and dry it before the fire when it is done.

Stuffing for Turkey.

Mix thoroughly a quart of stale bread, very finely grated; the grated rind of a lemon; quarter of an ounce of minced parsley and thyme, one part thyme, two parts parsley; and pepper and salt to season. Add to these one unbeaten egg and half a cup of butter; mix all well together and moisten with hot

38

water or milk. Other herbs than parsley or thyme may be used if preferred, and a little onion finely minced, added if desired.

Dumplings.

Put a pint of flour in a bowl; add a half teaspoonful of salt, and a rounding teaspoonful of baking powder; sift once or twice, add a little over a half cup of milk, the dough must be moist but not wet; drop this by spoonfuls over the top of the ragout, cover the saucepan and cook continuously for ten minutes without lifting the lid. Dish the dumplings around the edge of the platter and put the meat in the center.

New England Dinner.

Whenever your meet a native, or his descendant, of good old New England, you will find a being capable of appreciating a boiled dinner. Whether you select a small sugar-cured ham—really a shoulder, of course—weighing three or four pounds, or corned beef, or salt pork, there are important points to be observed in cooking meats and vegetables.

The "dinner" need not include the entire array of vegetables. For our purpose we will use potatoes, turnips, carrots and cabbage. It is a good plan to cook the meat early enough to admit of liquor cooling and removal of excess of fat before cooking the vegetables. Using corned beef, select a choice cut of three or four pounds, wash and soak in cold water and put on to cook in fresh, cold water. Skim, and simmer, until tender. Let it cool in liquor, remove the fat, reheat and use part of liquor in which to cook the turnips, carrots and potatoes in a separate kettle. Cut these vegetables in attractive pieces and arrange for cooking so that all will be done, and not overdone, at the same time. Cook the cabbage alone. Cut the head into eighths or sixteenths, according to size, or shred coarsely, have crisp by soaking in cold water, and cook in rapidly, salted water, uncovered, for twenty-five to thirty minutes, until tender. In serving, place meat in center of the platter, surrounded with cabbage as a bed for other vegetables, and arranged with some thought of attractiveness. Dust lightly with paprika, to aid digestion, and, if possible, introduce some bits of parsley as a garnish, of which it would be wise to partake. The meat and vegetables thus cooked with reference to digestibility, afford a boiled dinner that need not be paid for twice.

BEEF.

To Make Tough Meat Tender.

Soak it in vinegar and water; if a very large piece, for about twelve hours. For ten pounds of beef use three quarts of water to three-quarters of a pint of vinegar, and soak it for six or seven hours.

To Boil Beef.

Reckon the time from the water coming to a boil. Keep the pot boiling, but let it boil very slowly. If you let the pot cease boiling, you will be deceived in your time; therefore, watch that it does not stop, and keep up a good fire. Just before the pot boils the scum rises. Be sure to skim it off carefully, or it will fall back and adhere to the meat and disfigure it sadly. When you have well skimmed the pot, put in a little cold water, which will cause the scum to rise again. The more carefully you skim the cleaner and nicer the meat boiled will look.

Put your meat into cold water; a quart of cold water to every pound of meat. Allow twenty minutes to the pound from the time the pot boils and the scum rises. . It is more profitable to boil than to roast meat.

Kidney Stew. .

Time, two hours and a quarter.—Take a large beef kidney, cut all the fat out, cut it up in slices; then let it lay in cold water, with a teaspoonful of salt added, fifteen minutes; wipe dry, then put it in the pot with three half pints of cold water; let it boil two hours; half an hour before it is done add one large onion, sliced; one teaspoonful of powdered sage, and pepper and salt to season well; serve hot with mashed potatoes.

Stuffed Corned Beef.

Time, three hours.—Take a piece of well-corned rump or round, nine or ten pounds; make several deep cuts in it; fill with a stuffing of a handful of soaked bread, squeezed dry, a little fat or butter, a good pinch of cloves, allspice, pepper, a little finely chopped onion, and a little marjoram or thyme; then tie it up tightly in a cloth and saturate it with vinegar; boil about three hours.

Beef a-la-Mode.

. Time, three and a half hours.—Take a piece of meat, cross-rib is best, put a slice of bacon or some lard in the bottom of the pot, then the meat, and fill up with water till the meat is

41

covered; then take two onions, some pepper-corns, cloves, bay leaves, one carrot, and a crust of brown bread, salt and some vinegar; throw all this in over the beef, keep the pot well covered; fill up with more hot water if it boils down, and let it boil three hours; then burn a tablespoonful of flour, with some butter, a nice brown, thin with the gravy, and let it boil up once more with the meat; then put the beef in a deep dish and strain the gravy over it; add more vinegar to taste, serve with fried potatoes and red cabbage.

An English Stew of Cold Roast Beef.

Time, fifteen mines.—Cut the meat in small and rather thin slices, season them highly with salt and pepper, and dip each lightly in bread crumbs moistened in gravy or melted butter. Dress them neatly on a dish, and lay over them a thin layer of cut pickles, and moisten the whole with a glassful of pickled vinegar and the preserved gravy of the roast beef; heat in a Dutch oven and garnish with fried sippets or potato balls.

Boiled Bullock's Head.

Time to boil, five hours.—This is a good dish for a large family. Place the head in salt water for six hours, to cleanse it; then wash and remove the palates, and place them again in salt and water; put the head in a saucepan, with sufficient water to cover, boil for five hours, adding two carrots, two turnips, and two onions, cut small; when done, remove the head from the soup, and remove the bone from the meat; serve soup and meat in tureen; the palates, when white, boiled until tender, then pressed until cold, make a delicious relish for lunch or supper.

Broiled Steak.

For broiling, select only the choicest cuts from one inch to one and a half inches thick, remove bone and surplus fat, trim edges and skewer into shape. Have broiler very hot, grease with bit of suet and place steak close to flame to sear the surface. Turn, sear other side quickly and reduce flame or lower broiler and cook more slowly. Allow eight to ten minutes for steak one inch thick. Serve on hot platter, pour over part of fat, season and garnish. If a sauce should be desired use mushroom or maitre d'hotel or a "Clubhouse" seasoning. Never pierce meat with fork while cooking.

A Rolled, Stuffed Steak.

An inexpensive roast is from a large steak cut from best of round, about one and a half inches thick, scored, brushed with oil and vinegar, covered with a well seasoned stuffing of bread crumbs and rolled into a duck-shaped loaf. Dust with salt, pepper and flour, lay thin slices of suet and strips of fat, salt pork over the top, put in covered baking pan, add one cup of hot water and cook in moderately slow oven until tender. Nice hot or cold. Brown, mushroom, horseradish or flemish sauce may be served with it.

To Accompany Roast Beef.

A "tasty" adjunct to roasts with good brown sauce is mashed potato pie. Butter a shallow baking dish from which the pie may be served at the table, coat lightly with fine bread crumbs, fill with well mashed and seasoned potatoes, whipped until light, put on a pastry crust and bake as a pie. Serve with the roast, cutting in pie-shaped pieces and adding a spoonful or two of brown sauce.

Braised Beef.

Time, two hours; twelve persons.—Four pounds of beef, one carrot, one turnip, two tablespoonfuls of butter, one rounding teaspoonful of salt, one root of celery, two tablespoonfuls of flour, one salt spoonful of pepper. Purchase a piece of beef either from the round or from the shoulder cut the carrot and turnip into slices and then into blocks or dice. Cut the celery into small pieces; put the beef in a baking pan, put around the vegetables, add the pepper, pour this over the meat, cover the pan and cook in a slow oven one and a half to two hours, add the salt when the meat is half done. When the meat is done, lift it to the center of a large platter. Rub the butter and flour together, add it to the liquor in the pan which should now measure a pint; stir until boiling. Lift the vegetables carefully, arrange them neatly at the ends of the platter, strain over the sauce and send at once to the table. Serve with this either baked sweet or white potatoes.

Fricassee of Cold Beef.

Time, ten minutes.—Cut away all skin, gristle and fat; cut the meat in thin small slices; have ready a sauce made of stock thickened with butter rolled in flour, seasoned with shred parsley and young onions, pepper and salt. Strain the sauce when it is well flavored, and just heat the meat in it, soaking by the side of the fire; add a glass of red wine, the yolk of an egg well beaten and the juice of a lemon, stir for a few minutes, but do not let it boil or, like all rewarmed things, it will harden.

Beef Tongue (Corned or Smoked).

Soak the tongue twenty-four hours before boiling. It will require from three to four hours, according to size. The skin should always be removed as soon as it is taken from the pot. An economical method is to lay the tongue, as soon as the skin is removed, in a jar, coiled up with the tip outside the root, and a weight upon it. When it is cold, loosen the sides with a knife, and turn it out.

Beef Stewed with Onions.

Time, two hours and twenty minutes.—Cut two pounds of tender beef into small pieces, season with pepper and salt; slice one or two onions and add to it, with water enough to make a gravy. Let it stew slowly till the beef is thoroughly cooked, then add some pieces of butter rolled in flour, enough to make a rich gravy. Cold beef may be cooked in the same way, but the onions must then be cooked before adding them to the meat. Add more boiling water if it dries too fast.

Boiled Corned Beef.

Wash it well, put it in a pot and if very salt cover well with cold water; if only slightly corned, use boiling water; skim often while boiling, and allow at least half an hour for every pound of meat. If it is to be eaten cold, do not remove as soon as done, but allow it to remain in the liquor until nearly cold; then lay it in an earthen dish with a piece of board upon it and press with a stone or a couple of flat irons.

Savory Beef.

Take a shin of beef from the hind quarter, saw it into four pieces, put it in a pot and boil it until the meat and gristle drop from the bones; chop the meat very fine, put it in a dish and season it with a little salt, pepper, clove and sage, to your taste; pour in the liquor in which the meat was boiled and place it away to harden; cut in slices and serve cold.

Hash Balls of Corned Beef.

Prepare the hash by mincing with potatoes; make it into flat cakes; heat the griddle, and grease it with plenty of sweet butter; brown the balls first on one side and then on the other, and serve hot.

44

Tripe.

Must be washed in warm water and cut into squares of three inches; take one egg, three tablespoonfuls of flour, a little salt and make a thick batter by adding milk; fry out some slices of pork, dip the tripe into the batter and fry a light brown.

Beef Balls.

Take a piece of beef boiled tender, chop it very finely with an onion, season with salt and pepper, add parsley, bread crumbs, lemon peel and grated nutmeg; moisten it with an egg, mix well together, and roll it into balls. Then dip them in flour and fry them in boiling lard or fresh dripping. Serve them with thickened brown gravy, or fried bread crumbs.

Beef Liver.

Slice the liver and pour boiling water over it; wipe dry and cut it into very small pieces. Fry slices of fat, salt pork until brown; take out the pork and fry the liver in the fat; cook thoroughly. When done pour a little water over the liver and thicken with a little flour and water, mixed smooth. Salt to taste.

Stewed Shin of Beef.

Time, four hours and a quarter.—Saw the bone into three or four pieces, put them into a stewpan, and just cover them with cold water. When the pot simmers, skim it clean; and then add the sweet herbs, one large onion, celery, twelve black pepper-corns and twelve allspice. Stew it very gently over a slow fire till the meat is tender. Then peel the carrots and turnips and cut them into shapes; boil them with twelve small button onions till tender. The turnips and onions will take a quarter of an hour to boil, the carrots half an hour. Drain them carefully. Put the meat, when done, on a dish and keep it warm while you prepare some gravy, thus: Take a teacupful of the liquor in which the meat has been stewed and mix with it three tablespoonfuls of flour; add more liquor till you have a pint and a half of gravy. Season with pepper, salt and a wine glass of mushroom catsup. Boil it up, skim off the fat and strain it through a sieve. Pour it over the meat and lay the vegetables round it.

Spiced Beef.

Time, according to weight.—Take the thin part of a piece of beef after the rib piece (called the flap) 'has been cut off, if any of the ends of the bones are left take them out. Rub it well with salt and let it lay in pickle two days; then take half an ounce each of mace, cloves, black pepper and Jamaica pepper and a little chopped parsley and spread the whole equally over the beef; roll it up neatly and tie it very tight. Set it in a stewpan over a moderate fire, and let it stew slowly till quite tender. Then press it well, and when cold it will be fit to serve. The spices are to be laid on whole.

Bubble and Squeak.

Time, twenty minutes.—Chop up and fry about one pound each of previously boiled cold potatoes and cabbage, with a little pepper, salt and a good large piece of butter. Set it aside to keep hot. Lightly fry some slices of cold boiled beef; put them in a hot dish, with alternate layers of vegetable, piling it higher in the middle.

Minced Beef.

Time, twenty minutes.—Mince about a pound and a half of beef with six ounces of bacon and two onions, seasoning it highly with pepper and nutmeg. Take a sufficient quantity of stock made from bones, and any trimmings, a piece of butter rolled in flour, and a little browning; make it hot and strain it over the mince; put the whole into a stewpan, let it simmer for a few minutes, and serve it on a hot dish with sippets of toasted bread and a poached or hard-boiled egg divided and placed on each sippet arranged round the edge of dish. It is also served surrounded by a wall of mashed potatoes, with two poached eggs lying on the top of it.

Beef Stew.

Take three pounds of beef—navel piece is the best—cut in inch square pieces; peel and slice four or five onions; put a layer of meat in the bottom of the pot, then a layer of onions, and so on until used up; season each layer with pepper and salt; cover with boiling water; boil slowly and keep the pot covered. Peel a quart of potatoes, cut into small pieces; add the potatoes about half an hour before serving.

Hash.

Take cold pieces of beef that have been left over and chop them fine; then add cold boiled potatoes chopped fine; add pepper and salt and a little warm water; put all in a frying-pan and cook slowly for twenty minutes.

46

Baked Calves' Hearts.

Time, two hours; six persons.—Two calves' hearts, one cupful of bread crumbs, one tablespoonful of melted butter, one teaspoonful of salt, one quart of boiling water, one salt spoonful of pepper. Wash the hearts in cold water; make a stuffing from the bread crumbs, melted butter, salt and pepper. Cut the tubes from the upper part of the hearts and put in the stuffing; sew the tops, and stand them in a stewing pan. tips down; cover the pan, and stew slowly one hour. Then put them in a baking pan, baste with melted butter, and bake one hour. Dish the hearts, the points toward the center of the dish; remove the strings, and fill the bottom of the dish with nicely seasoned peas. Pass with them a brown sauce made from the water in which the hearts were stewed.

MUTTON.

Stuffed Leg of Mutton.

Boil two large white onions until tender, then chop fine; add bread crumbs and sage to taste, a little salt and pepper; then slit the sinewy part of the leg and insert the stuffing and roast.

Mutton Cutlets.

Take a piece of the best end of a neck of mutton, saw off the bones short, remove the gristle and fat, cut the cutlets about one-third of an inch in thickness, shape and trim them neatly; beat them with a cutlet bat dipped in water; pepper, salt and broil them over a brisk fire.

Irish Stew.

Time, two hours and a half.—Put two pounds of mutton cutlets or chops and four pounds good potatoes, peeled and sliced, in alternate layers in a large saucepan or stewpan, season to taste with pepper and salt, and a finely shred onion; add a pint of cold water, and simmer gently for two hours. Serve very hot.

Mutton Sausage.

Take a cold roast mutton, cut it in as large slices as possible; then take bread crumbs, sweet herbs, salt and pepper, wet them with an egg and put a small quantity into the center of each slice; roll each slice by itself, and tie it up as tightly as possible; cook them in hot melted butter or beef drippings until brown and crisp.

47

Roast Shoulder of Mutton.

Time, a quarter of an hour to each pound.—Take out the bone and fill the space with a stuffing made of bread crumbs, salt pork chopped fine, pepper, salt and sage, or sweet marjoram.

Stewed Leg of Mutton.

Time, two hours.—Make a stuffing of finely chopped beef suet, bread crumbs, an onion chopped finely, pepper, salt and a little ground clove. Make incisions in the leg and stuff it well; tie a little bundle of basil and parsley together; lay in the bottom of the pot and on it place the mutton; just cover with water and stew slowly for two hours; when tender, take out the mutton and add to the liquor a large spoonful of flour, made smooth with a little water, stir it well, and in five minutes take it off and strain it; pour it back into the pot and add a wine glassful of catsup and lay the mutton in till it is served.

Boiled Leg of Lamb.

Time, about one hour and a quarter.—Boil it in water to cover it; when half done add two cups of milk to the water, with a large spoonful of salt. It should be served with spinach and caper sauce.

To Fry Lamb Steaks.

Dip each piece into well-beaten egg, cover with bread crumbs or corn meal and fry in butter or new lard. Serve with mashed potatoes and boiled rice. Thicken the gravy with flour and butter, adding a little lemon juice, and pour it hot upon the steaks, and place the rice in spoonfuls around the dish to garnish it.

Cold Mutton Broiled.

Time, five minutes.—Cut in thick slices cold boiled leg of mutton; it should not be cooked too much or it will fall into pieces; salt and pepper it and then broil. Serve very hot, and add a thick sauce flavored with fresh tomatoes or tomato sauce.

Lamb or Mutton Stew.

Time, two hours and a quarter.—Part of a breast of mutton or lamb, cut in bits as many potatoes, pepper and salt to taste, two onions, a bunch of parsley, a bunch of sweet herbs. Stew all together in sufficient water to cover them for two hours gently. Then put in a teacupful of tomato catsup and boil up again. Serve hot.

VEAL.

Prepared Veal.

Mince three pounds, raw (best parts), of a leg of veal, fat and lean, take six butter-crackers, pounded fine, two eggs, butter size of an egg, teaspoonful pepper and one of ground cloves, tablespoonful salt, a little parsley, one slice salt pork, chopped fine. Work well together, make into the form of a loaf, put bits of butter on top, put in dripping pan with water in it and bake two hours in oven, basting often with the water; try it with fork to see if done. This is eaten cold and is a capital dish for lunch, etc., to be cut in slices when helped. It is called prepared veal. Chicken may be used, or any meat, but veal is best.

Eggs and Minced Veal.

Take some remnants of roast veal, trim off all the browned parts and mince it very finely; fry a shallot, chopped small, in plenty of butter; when it is a light straw color add a large pinch of flour and a little stock; then the minced meat with chopped parsley, pepper, salt and nutmeg to taste; mix well, add more stock if necessary, and let the mince gradually get hot by the side of the fire; lastly add a few drops of lemon juice. Serve with sippets of bread, fried in butter round, and poached eggs on top.

Veal Loaf.

Time pounds of uncooked veal, quarter of a pound of pork; chop these fine; add two eggs, one cupful pounded crackers, one teaspoonful of salt, two of pepper; sage and summer savory to suit the taste; press hard in a pudding-dish and bake one and a half hours; cut in thin slices when cold.

Calf's Head, Boiled.

Time to soak, two hours; to simmer, two hours.—Let the butcher split the head in halves. Take out the eyes and the snout bone; then lay it in cold water to soak two hours before boiling; take out the brains and wash them well in several waters, then lay them in cold water. Put the heads together and lay it in a good sized pot; cover it with cold water and throw in a tablespoonful of salt; let it boil slowly for two or three hours. When it has boiled a little more than an hour, take about a quart of the liquor and put into a stewpan for the gravy; add to it some salt, pepper, a little parsley chopped fine, a tablespoonful of lemon pickle, and then boil. Beat up an egg lightly, with two tablespoonfuls of flour, then remove care-

fully the skin from the brains and beat them up with the egg
and flour. When well beaten thicken the gravy with it and
stew about ten minutes.

Roast Veal.

Time, three hours.—Make a dressing of bread crumbs,
chopped thyme and parsley; a little pepper and salt, one egg
and a little butter. If too dry moisten with a little hot water.
Take a loin of veal, make an incision in the flap and fill it with
the stuffing; secure it with small skewers and dredge the veal
with a little flour, slightly salted. Bake in a moderate oven
and baste often; at first with a little salt and water, and afterward with the drippings in the pan. When done, skim the gravy
and thicken with a little brown flour. The breast and shoulder
are nice cooked in the same manner; ask your butcher to make
incisions for the stuffing. Serve with tomato sauce.

Veal Minced.

Time, one hour and a quarter altogether.—Mince the veal
as finely as possible, separating the skin, gristle and bones, with
which a gravy should be made. Put a small quantity of the
gravy into a stewpan, with a little lemon peel grated, and a
spoonful of milk or cream. Thicken it with a little butter and
flour, mix gradually with the gravy; season it with salt and
a little lemon juice and cayenne pepper. Put in the minced
veal and let it simmer a few minutes. Serve it upon sippets
of toasted bread.

Knuckle of Veal

Time, two hours and three-quarters.—Cut in small thick
slices, season with a little salt and pepper, flour lightly and
fry it to a pale brown, then lay it in a saucepan and cover with
water. Skim well and season with thyme and parsley and a
little mace. Simmer gently for two hours and a half, then
thicken the gravy with a little flour and add a piece of butter
and salt to taste. Add a little catsup if desired.

Spiced Veal.

Time, one hour.—One pound of veal, chopped very fine;
season with two well-beaten eggs, a tablespoonful of butter, teaspoonful of salt and sage each. Put it into a cake-pan, and bake
about an hour. Slice when cold.

Fried Sweet Breads.

For every mode of dressing they should be prepared by
half boiling, and then putting them in cold water; this makes

50

them whiter and firmer. Dip them in beaten eggs and then into bread crumbs; pepper and salt and fry in lard. Serve with peas or tomatoes.

Stewed Sweet Breads.

Time, thirty-five minutes.—After they are parboiled and cold, lard them with fat pork; put them in a stewpan, with some good veal gravy and juice of a small lemon; stew them till very tender, and just before serving thicken with flour and butter; serve them with the gravy.

Calf's Brains and Tongue.

Time, to boil ten or fifteen minutes.—Separate the two lobes of the brain with a knife, soak them in cold water with a little salt in it for an hour; then pour away the cold water and cover them with hot water; clean and skin them. Boil them then very gently in half a pint of water, take off the scum carefully as it rises. Take them up, drain and chop them and put them to warm in a stewpan with the herbs chopped, the melted butter or cream, and the seasoning. Squeeze a little lemon juice over them; stir them well together. Boil the tongue; skin it; take off the roots; lay it in the middle of the dish and serve the brains around it.

Veal Cutlets.

Time, twelve to fifteen minutes.—Let the cutlet be about half an inch thick, and cut it into pieces the size and shape of a crown piece. Chop some sweet herbs very fine; mix them well with the bread crumbs. Brush the cutlets over with the yolk of an egg, then cover them with the bread crumbs and chopped herbs; fry them lightly in butter, turning them when required. Take them out when done. Mix an ounce of fresh butter with the grated peel of half a lemon, a little nutmeg and flour; pour a little water into the frying-pan and stir the butter, flour and grated lemon peel into it; then put the cutlets ino this gravy to heat. Serve them piled in the center of the dish with thin rolls of bacon as a garnish.

Calf's Liver and Bacon.

Time, quarer of an hour.—Soak two or three livers in cold water for half an hour, then dry it in a cloth, and cut it into thin, narrow slices; take about a pound of bacon, or as much as you may require, and cut an equal number of thin slices as you have of liver; fry the bacon lightly, take it out and keep it hot; then fry the liver in the same pan, seasoning it with

51

pepper and salt, and dredge over it a little flour. When it is a nice brown, arrange it round the dish with a roll of bacon between each slice. Pour off the fat from the pan, put in about two ounces of butter well rubbed in flour to thicken the gravy; squeeze in the juice of a lemon and add a cupful of hot water; boil it, and pour it into the center of the dish. Serve it garnished with forcemeat balls or slices of lemon.

PORK.

To Roast a Leg of Pork.

Time, twenty minutes to one pound.—The leg to be roasted should not weigh more than six or seven pounds. Score the rind or skin with a sharp knife all round the joint. Baste it well. It will yield sufficient dripping to baste itself without butter. If the crackling and fat are not kept on, the joint will not require so long a time to roast it. Sauce: Brown gravy or tomato.

To Steam a Ham.

Time, twenty minutes to each pound.—If the ham has been hung for some time, put it into cold water, and let it soak all night, or let it lie on a damp stone sprinkled with water for two days to mellow. Wash it well, put it into a steamer—there are proper ones made for the purpose—over a pot of boiling water. Steam it for as long a time as the weight requires, the proportion of time given above.

This is by far the best way of cooking a ham. It prevents waste and retains the flavor. When it is done, skin it and strew bread-raspings over it as usual. If you preserve the skin as whole as possible and cover the ham when cold with it, it will prevent its becoming dry.

To Boil a Ham.

Time, four or five hours.—Well soak the ham in a large quantity of water for twenty-four hours, then trim and scrape it very clean, put it into a large stewpan with more than sufficient water to cover it; put in a blade of mace; a few cloves, a sprig of thyme and two bay leaves. Boil it four or five hours, according to its weight; and when done, let it become cold in the liquor in which it was boiled. Then remove the rind carefully without injuring the fat, press a cloth over it to absorb as much of the grease as possible, and shake some bread-raspings over the fat, or brush it thickly over with glaze. Serve.

it cold, garnished with parsley, or aspic jelly in the dish. Ornament the knuckle with a paper frill and vegetable flowers.

To Bake a Ham.

Time, four hours.—Take a medium sized ham and place it to soak for ten or twelve hours. Then cut away the rusty part from underneath, wipe it dry, and cover it rather thickly over with a paste of flour and water. Put it into an earthen dish, and set it in a moderately heated oven for four hours. When done, take off the crust carefully and peel off the skin, put a frill of cut paper round the knuckle, and raspings of bread over the fat of the ham, or serve it glazed, and garnished with cut vegetables.

To Boil a Leg of Pork.

Time, a quarter of an hour for each pound, and half an hour over.—Procure a nice small compact leg of pork, rub it well with salt, and let it remain for a week in pickle, turning and rubbing the pickle into it once a day. Let it lie for half an hour in cold water before it is dressed to improve the color; then put it into a large pot or stewpan and well cover it with water. Let it boil gradually, and skim frequently as the scum rises. On no account let it boil fast, or the meat will be hardened, and the knuckle end will be done before the thick part. When done, serve it on a hot dish with a garnish of turnips or parsnips.

To Boil Bacon.

Time, one hour and a half for two or three pounds.—If very salt, soak it in soft water two hours before cooking. Put it into a saucepan with plenty of water and let it boil gently. If a fine piece of the gammon of bacon, it may, when done, have the skin, as in hams, stripped off, and have finely powdered bread-raspings strewed over it.

Ham.

Boil the ham till well cooked. Take it out of the water and drain till cold. When cold remove the outside skin and make slight incisions in the fat on the top of ham with a knife. Sprinkle three or four tablespoonfuls of powdered moist sugar over the top of the ham. Roast in oven for twenty minutes, basting about every five minutes with a pint of cooking sherry. Remove from the oven while doing so, using the sherry enough at a time to baste thoroughly with it.

Pig's Tongues.

Partially boil the tongue in order to remove the skin. Pickle them as you would pickle a ham; lay them one on the top of each other under a heavy weight. Cover the pan in which you place them, and let them remain for a week, then dry them, and put them into sausage skins. Fasten them up at the ends and smoke them.

To Roast a Pig's Head.

Time to roast, half an hour.—Boil it tender enough to take the bones out. Then chop some sage fine, mix it with the pepper and salt, and rub it over the head. Hang it on the split, and roast it at a good fire. Baste it well. Make a good gravy and pour over it. Apple sauce is eaten with it.

Pig's Head Boiled.

Time, one hour and a half.—This is the more, profitable dish, though not so pleasant to the palate; it should first be salted, which is usually done by the pork butcher; it should be boiled gently. Serve with vegetables.

Pig's Cheek.

Time, three-quarters of an hour.—Boil and trim in the shape of ham, and if very fat carve it as a cockle-shell; glaze it well, or put over it bread crumbs and brown them.

To Fricassee Pork.

Cut a small sparerib or chine of pork into pieces, cover with water and stew until tender; remove the meat and flavor the gravy with salt, pepper, and thicken with a little flour. Serve in a deep dish, in the gravy, and garnish the dish with rice.

Ham and Eggs.

Chop finely some cold boiled ham, fat and lean together, say a pound to four eggs; put a piece of butter in the pan, then the ham; let it get well warmed through, then beat the eggs light; stir them in briskly.

Corned Pork.

Time, four hours.—It should be soaked a few hours before boiling, then washed and scraped, and put into fresh water. It must not be boiled fast, but put into cold water and gradually warmed through; skim frequently while boiling.

A leg or shoulder weighing seven or eight pounds should

boil slowly for four hours. When taken up it must be skinned carefully, though some prefer the skin remaining on, as it loses much of the juice by skinning. It is very nice cold.

Pork Chops.

Time, fifteen minutes.—Cut the chops about half an inch thick, and trim them neatly; put a frying-pan on the fire, with a bit of butter; as soon as it is hot, put in your chops, turning them often till brown all over; a few minutes before they are done, season with powdered sage, pepper and salt.

Ham Toast.

Mix with one tablespoonful of finely chopped or grated ham, the beaten-up yolk of an egg, and a little cream and pepper; heat over the fire, and then spread the mixture either on hot buttered toast, or on slices of bread fried quite crisp in butter; serve very hot.

Saveloys.

Time, half an hour to bake.—Remove the skin and bone from six pounds of young pork, and salt it with one ounce of saltpetre and one pound of common salt; let it stand in the pickle for three days and then mince it up very fine, and season it with three teaspoonfuls of pepper and twelve sage leaves chopped as small as possible; add to it one pound of grated bread, and mix it all well together; fill the skins and bake them in a slow oven for half an hour. They may be eaten hot or cold.

MEAT PIES AND PUDDINGS.

We give general directions on this most important art. First, the cook should have smooth cold hands—very clean—for making paste or crust. She should wash them well and plunge them in cold water for a minute or two in hot weather, drying them well afterwards before beginning her paste.

Be very careful about the proper heat of the oven for baking pies, as if it be too cold the paste will be heavy and have a dull look; if too hot, the crust will burn before the pie is done.

Try if the oven is hot enough by holding your hand inside it for a few seconds; if you can do so without snatching it out again quickly, it is too cold; it is best, however, to try it by baking a little piece of the crust in it first.

Always make a small hole with the knife at the top of the

pie to allow the gases generated in it by the cooking to escape. This aperture is also useful for pouring gravy into the pie when it is done, if more is required.

To Clarify Beef Dripping.

Put the dripping into a basin, pour over it some boiling water, and stir it round with a silver spoon; set it to cool, and then remove the dripping from the sediment, and put it into basins or jars for use in a cool place. Clarified dripping may be used for frying and basting everything excepting game or poultry, as well as for pies, etc.

To Make a Short Crust With Dripping.

One pound of flour, three-quarters of a pound of clarified beef dripping, one wineglassful of very cold water, a pinch of salt.

Take care that the water you use is cold, especially in summer. Put the flour, well dried, into a large basin (which should be kept for the purpose) with a pinch of salt; break up the clarified beef dripping into pieces and mix them well with the flour, rubbing both together until you have a fine powder. Then make a hole in the middle of the flour and pour in water enough to make a smooth and flexible paste. Sprinkle the pasteboard with flour, and your hands also, take out the lump of paste, roll it out, fold it together again and roll it out— i. e., roll it three times, the last time it should be of the thickness required for your crust, that is, about a quarter of an inch, or even thinner. It is then ready for use.

Common Puff Paste.

Put one pound of sifted flour on the slab, or in an earthen basin; make a hollow in the center, work into it a quarter of a pound of lard and half a teaspoonful of salt. When it is mixed through the flour, add as much cold water as will bind it together, then a little flour over the pasteboard or table; flour the rolling-pin, and roll out the paste to half an inch in thickness; divide half a pound of butter in three parts, spread one evenly over the paste, fold it up, dredge a little flour over it and the paste-slab or table, roll it out again, spread another portion of the butter over, and fold and roll again, so continue until all the butter is used; roll it out to a quarter of an inch in thickness for use.

56

Suet Crust for Puddings.

One pound of flour, six ounces of beef suet, a cupful of cold water. Strip the skin from the suet, chop it as fine as possible, rub it well into the flour, mix it with a knife, work it to a very smooth paste with a cupful of water and roll it out for use.

Game Pie.

Time to bake, about two hours.—"Raise" a crust to a size corresponding with the quantity of your game. Cut with a sharp knife the flesh from the best parts; keep each kind separate, and set them aside for a moment. Then split the heads, break the bones, and put them with the inferior parts into a stewpan, with a roasted onion, a carrot, a teaspoonful of salt, twenty black peppercorns, sprigs of winter savory, marjoram, lemon and common thyme, two bay leaves, half a clove of garlic and half a pound of gravy beef. Stew in a very little water (according to the quantity of the meat) five hours. When done, skim and strain, and set it aside to cool. Line the whole of your raised crust with a thin layer of short paste, then a layer of fat bacon or ham cut in thin slices. Now put in your different kinds of game in layers, not round, but from the bottom, filling up the corners and crevices with forcemeat stuffing. Having mixed together two teaspoonfuls of salt, have a teaspoonful of cayenne, and half a grated nutmeg; sprinkle a little of them over each layer. Finish the filling with a layer of ham or bacon; put over it a layer of the short paste; then cover with the raised crust. Pinch round the sides, ornament by crimping leaves set according to fancy, and bake in a moderate oven an hour, an hour and a half or two hours, according to size. When both pie and gravy are nearly cold put the point of a funnel into the small hole (which, by the way, you must make in the top of the pie before you bake it), and gently pour through it the gravy you have prepared.

Potato Patsy.

Time, nearly two hours.—Cut about a pound and a half of beefsteak into thin slices, season it with pepper and salt to taste, lay it at the bottom of a Pedro-pan, and put small pieces of butter on the top, pour in a large cupful of stock or gravy and put in the perforated plate. Mash some fine mealy potatoes with a few spoonfuls of milk, and fill up the whole space to the top of the tube of the pan, press the potato down, and mark it with a knife in any form you please. Bake it in a

57

moderate oven a delicate color. Send it to the table with a folded napkin round it and when served lift up the plate off potatoes.

Plain Beefsteak Pie.

Time, one hour and a half.—Cut two and a half pounds of steak into small pieces with a very little fat, dip each piece into flour, place them in a pie-dish, seasoning each layer with pepper, salt and a very little cayenne pepper, fill the dish sufficiently with slices of steak to raise the crust in the middle, half fill the dish with water or any gravy left from roast beef, and a spoonful of Worcestershire sauce; put a border of paste round the wet edge of the pie dish; moisten it and lay the crust over it. Cut the paste even with the edge of the pie dish all round, ornament it with leaves of paste, and brush it over with the beaten yolk of an egg. Make a hole with a knife in the top, and bake it in a hot oven.

Mutton Pie.

Time to bake, one hour and a half or two hours.—Strip the meat from the bones of a loin of mutton without dividing it, and cut it into nice thin slices, and season them with pepper and salt; put a pie crust round the edge of a pie-dish, place in it a layer of mutton, then one of forcemeat, and again the slices of mutton with three or four halves of kidneys at equal distances; then pour in a gravy made from the bones seasoned and well cleared from fat. Moisten the edge with water. Cover with a paste half an inch thick; press it round with your thumbs, make a hole in the center, and cut the edges close to the dish, ornament the top and border according to your taste, and bake it.

Veal and Oyster Pie.

Time to bake, one hour and a half.—Cut a pound and a half of veal into small neat cutlets, and spread over each a thin layer of minced or pounded ham, season them with pepper, salt, and grated lemon peel, and roll each cutlet round. Line the edge of a pie-dish with a good paste, put a layer of rolled veal at the bottom, over the veal a layer of oysters, then of veal, and the oysters on the top; make a gravy with a cupful of weak gravy or broth, the peel of half a lemon, the oyster liquor strained, and a seasoning of peper and salt; cover a crust over the top; ornament it in any way approved, egg it over, and bake it in a moderate oven. When done, more gravy may be

58

added by pouring it through the hole on the top through a funnel, and replacing an ornament on it after the gravy is added.

Cheshire Pork Pie.

Time, one hour and a half.—Take the skin and fat from a loin of pork, and cut it into thin steaks; season them with pepper, salt and nutmeg; line a pie-dish with paste, put in a layer of pork, then of pippins pared and cored, and about two ounces of sugar; then place in another layer of pork, and half a pint of white wine, and lay some butter on the top; cover it over with puff paste, pass a knife through the top to leave an opening, cut the paste even with the dish, egg it once and bake it.

A Plain Rabbit Pie.

Time to bake, one hour and a quarter.—Skin and wash a fine large rabbit; cut it into joints and divide the head. Then place it in warm water to soak until thoroughly clean; drain it on a sieve, or wipe it with a clean cloth. Season it with pepper and salt, a sprig of parsley chopped fine, and one shallot if the flavor is liked (but it is equally good without it). Cut the bacon into small pieces, dredge the rabbit with flour, and place it with the bacon in a pie-dish, commencing with the inferior parts of the rabbit. Pour in a small cupful of water, or stock if you have it; put a paste border round the edges of the dish, and cover it with a puff paste about half an inch thick. Ornament and glaze the top, make a hole in the center and bake it.

A Plain Pigeon Pie.

Time to bake, one hour and a quarter.—Lay a rim of paste round the sides and edge of a pie-dish, sprinkle a little pepper and salt over the bottom and put in a thin beefsteak; pick and draw the pigeons, wash them clean, cut off the feet, and press the legs into the sides; put a bit of butter and a seasoning of pepper and salt in the inside of each, and lay them in the dish with their breasts upwards, and the necks and gizzrads between them; sprinkle some pepper and salt over them and put in a wine glass of water; lay a thin sheet of paste over the top, and with a brush wet it all over; then put a puff paste half an inch thick over that, cut it close to the dish, brush it over with egg, ornament the top, and stick four of the feet out of it and bake it. When done, pour in a little good gravy. You may put in the yolks of six hard-boiled eggs, or leave out the beefsteak, if you think proper.

Veal and Ham Patties.

Time, a quarter of an hour.—Chop about six ounces of ready dressed lean veal, and three ounces of ham, very small, put it into a stewpan with an ounce of butter rolled in flour, a tablespoonful of cream, the same of veal stock, a little grated nutmeg and lemon peel, some cayenne pepper and salt, a spoonful of essence of ham and lemon juice. Mix all well together and stir it over the fire until quite hot, taking care it does not burn. Bake them in a hot oven for a quarter of an hour; fill with the mixture and serve.

Moulded Veal, or Veal Cakes.

Time, half an hour to bake.—Slices of cold roast veal; slices of ham; three eggs; some gravy; two sprigs of parsley; pepper and salt. Cut a few slices of ham and veal very thin, taking off the skin from the veal, chop two sprigs of parsley fine, and cut the eggs hard-boiled into slices. Take any nice shaped mould, butter it, and put the veal, ham, eggs and parsley in layers until the mould is full, seasoning each layer with a little pepper and salt, placing a few slices of egg at the bottom of the mould at equal distances, fill up with good stock and bake it. When cold turn it out, and serve on a folded napkin, garnished with flowers cut out of carrots, turnips, and a little parsley.

Beefsteak Pudding.

Time to boil, about two hours.—Put a pound, or a little more, of flour in a basin, and mix it thoroughly with some very finely chopped suet; put in a good heaped salt spoonful of salt. Mix it to a paste with water; flour the pasteboard, the roller and your hands. Take out the lump of paste and roll it out about half an inch thick. Butter a round-bottomed pudding-basin, line it with paste, turning a little over the edge. Cut up the steak into small pieces, with a little fat, flour them slightly, season them highly with peper and salt, then lay them in the basin, pour over them a gill of water. Roll out the rest of the paste, cover it over the top of the basin, pressing it down with the thumb. Tie the basin in a floured pudding-cloth, and put it in a saucepan in a gallon of boiling water, keep it continually boiling for nearly two hours, occasionally adding a little more water. Take it up, untie the cloth, turn the pudding over on the dish, and take the basin carefully from it. Serve.

Beefsteak and Kidney Pudding.

Time, to boil two hours.—Take a pound of nice tender beef and beef kidney, cut them into pieces about a quarter of an inch thick, season them with pepper and salt, and dredge a little flour over them. Lightly butter a round-bottomed pudding basin, roll out the paste to about half an inch in thickness and line the basin, then put in the beef and kidney, pour in three or four tablespoonfhls of water, cover a piece of paste over the top, press it firmly together with your thumb, then tie the pudding basin in a floured cloth, and put it into a saucepan with four quarts of water; keep it constantly boiling, adding more boiling water if required.

Mutton Pudding.

Time to boil, rather more than two hours.—Make a paste as for beefsteak pudding. Cut the meat in slices, season it with the herbs, pepper, and salt. Put a layer of meat in the basin, then one of slices of raw potatoes, till the basin is full. Cover it with the crust, tie it in a floured cloth and boil it in sufficient water.

Veal Pudding.

Time, one hour to boil.—Cut about two pounds of lean veal into small collops a quarter of an inch in thickness, put a piece of butter the size of an egg into a very clean frying-pan to melt, then lay in the veal and a few slices if bacon, a small sprig of thyme, and a seasoning of pepper and salt, place the pan over a slow fire for about ten minutes, then add two or three spoonfuls of warm water. Just boil it up, and then let it stand to cool. Line a pudding basin with a good suet crust, lay in the veal and bacon, pour the gravy over it, roll out a piece of paste to form a lid, place it over, press it close with the thumb, tie the basin in a pudding cloth, and put it into a saucepan of boiling water, keeping it continually boiling until done.

Rabbit Pudding.

Time, two hours to boil.—Cut a small rabbit into small neat pieces, and have ready a few slices of bacon or ham. Line a basin with a good suet crust. Lay in the pieces of rabbit with the bacon or ham intermixed, season to your taste with pepper and salt, and pour in a cupful of water. Cover the crust over the top, press it securely with the thumb and finger, and boil it.

Suet Pudding.

Time, to boil one hour and a quarter.—Mix one pound of flour very dry with half a pound of finely chopped suet, add eggs and a pinch of salt; make it into a paste with the water, beating it all rapidly together with a wooden spoon. Flour a pudding cloth, put the paste into it, tie the cloth tightly, and plunge it into the boiling water. The shape may be either a roll or a round ball. When it is done, untie the cloth, turn the pudding out, and serve very hot.

POULTRY.

To Roast Wild Fowl.

The flavor is best preserved without stuffing. Put pepper, salt and a piece of butter into each. Wild fowl require much less dressing than tame. A rich brown gravy should be sent in the dish; and when the breast is cut into slices, before taking off the bone, a squeeze of lemon, with pepper and salt, is a great improvement to the flavor. To take off the fishy taste which wild fowl sometimes have, put an onion, salt, and hot water into the dripping pan and baste them for the first ten minutes with this; then take away the pan and baste constantly with butter.

To Roast a Turkey.

Pluck the bird carefully and singe off the down with lighted paper, break the leg bone close to the foot and hang up the bird and draw out the strings from the thigh. Never cut the breast; make a slit down the back of the neck and take out the crop that way, then cut the neck bone close, and after the bird is stuffed the skin can be turned over the back and the crop will look full and round. Cut around the vent, making the opening as small as possible, and draw carefully, taking care that the gall bag and the gut joining the gizzard are not broken. Open the gizzard and remove the contents and detach the liver from the gall bladder. The liver, gizzard and heart, if used in the gravy, will need to be boiled an hour and a half and chopped as fine as possible. Wash the turkey and wipe thoroughly dry, inside and out; then fill the inside with stuff· ing and either sew the skin of the neck over the back or fasten it with a small skewer. Sew up the opening at the vent; then run a long skewer into the pinion and thigh through the body, passing it through the opposite pinion and thigh. Put a skewer in the small part of the leg, close on the outside of the sidesman, and push it through. Pass a string over the points of the skewers and tie it securely at the back.

Dredge well with flour, and cover the breast with nicely buttered white paper, place on a grating in the dripping pan and put in the oven to roast. Baste every fifteen minutes—a few times with butter and water, and afterward with gravy in the dripping pan. Do not have too hot an oven. A turkey weighing ten pounds will require nearly three hours to bake. Stew the giblets in just water enough to cover them, and when the turkey is lifted from the pan, add these (chopped very fine) with the water in which they were boiled, to the drippings; thicken with browned flour, boil up once and pour into the gravy boat. If the dripipngs are too fat, skim well before putting in the giblets. Serve with cranberry sauce, currant or apple jelly.

Roast Goose.

Geese and ducks, if old, are better parboiled before they are roasted. Put them on in sufficient water to cover them, and simmer about two hours. Make a stuffing with four onions, one ounce of green sage, chopped fine, a large cupful of stale bread-crumbs and the same of mashed potatoes, one teaspoonful of butter, a little pepper and salt, and one unbeaten egg; mix them well together and stuff the body of the goose; then place in the oven and bake about an hour and a half. Serve with apple sauce.

Roast Pigeons.

When cleaned and ready for roasting, fill the bird with a stuffing of bread-crumbs, a spoonful of butter, a little salt and nutmeg, and three oysters to each bird (some prefer chopped apple). They must be well basted with melted butter, and require thirty minutes' careful cooking. In the autumn they are best, and should be full grown.

Roast Duck.

Prepare your duck for roasting and use the following stuffing: Chop fine and throw into cold water three good-sized onions, one large spoonful of sage, two of bread-crumbs, a piece of butter the size of a walnut, a little salt and pepper, and the onions drained. Mix well together, and stuff the duck.

An hour is enough for an ordinary sized duck. The gravy is made by straining the dripping; skim off the fat, then stir in a large spoonful of browned flour, a teaspoonful of mixed mustard, a wineglassful of claret. Simmer for ten minutes.

63

Boiled Turkey.

Prepare your turkey as for roasting; put it in a cloth and boil it slowly, if from eight to nine pounds, an hour and a half. Throw into the water a few cloves, a little black pepper, sweet marjoram and salt. It is to be served with oysters. Skim the turkey well while boiling or it will not be white.

Chicken Fricassee.

Time, three hours and a quarter.—Prepare a couple of nice chickens; joint them, dividing the wings, side, breast and back-bone, and let them lie in salt and water half an hour, remove them then to a stewpan, with half a pound of good, sweet salt pork, cut up in pieces; barely cover with water, and simmer on top of the stove or range for three hours; when sufficiently tender, take out the chicken, mix a tablespoonful of flour smoothly with cold milk, and add a little fine dried or chopped parsley, sage and thyme or summer savory, and stir gradually into the liquor; keep stirring till it boils; season with pepper and salt to taste; and then put back the chicken and let it boil up for a few moments in the gravy; garnish with the green tops of celery.

Chicken Pot Pie.

Time, one hour.—Divide the chicken into pieces at the joints; boil until part done, or about twenty minutes, then take it out. Fry two or three slices of fat salt pork, and put in the bottom, then place the chicken on it with three pints of water, two ounces of butter, a teaspoonful of pepper, and cover over the top with a light crust, made the same as for biscuit.

Ragout of Ducks.

Put the gizzards, livers, necks, etc., into a pint of good strong beef broth, or other well seasoned stock. Season the ducks inside with salt and mixed spices. Brown them on all sides in a frying pan, and then stew them till tender in a strained stock. When nearly ready thicken the sauce with browned flour and butter.

Chicken Jelly.

Boil a pair of chickens until you can pull the meat from the bones; remove all the meat and allow the bones to boil half an hour longer; stand this in a cool place and it will become jellied; the next day cut the meat into small pieces, melt the jelly and throw it in; then add two tablespoonfuls of Worcestershire sauce, two of walnut sauce, one tablespoonful of salt, a pinch of powdered mace, cloves, and allspice; slice ten hard-boiled eggs and two lemons; line a large bowl or form with these slices, then pour in the mixture and let it stand in a cool place, but not to freeze. The water should just cover the chickens when put to boil. This is a very ornamental dish and keeps for a long time.

To Hash Ducks.

Nothing tastes better than a fat roast duck. Cut it into pieces as in carving at table, skin and soak these by the side of the fire in a little boiling gravy till thoroughly hot. Add a small glass of wine and a sufficient quantity of mixed spices to give the sauce a high relish.

Chicken Salad.

Boil a chicken; do not chop very fine; cut up one bunch of celery, the size of a cent; to make the dressing, wash smooth the yolk of a hard-boiled egg, one teaspoonful of salt, one or two tablespoonfuls of made mustard; stir in slowly four table-spoonfuls of sweet oil, then two tablespoonfuls of vinegar; pour over the chicken and celery.

Chicken Croquettes.

One large chicken, two sweet-breads, wine glass of cream, one loaf baker's stale bread. Cook chicken and sweet-bread separately, saving the chicken broth. Chop chicken, meat and sweet-bread finely together, season with pepper, salt, parsley, and half a teaspoonful grated onion. Rub the bread into crumbs until you have equal quantities of crumbs and meat. Place over the fire as much of the chicken broth as will moisten well the crumbs, into which stir the cream, and butter size of an egg. When it boils, stir in crumbs until they adhere to the spoon. Add meat, and, when cold, two well-beaten eggs. Mold into rolls, with your hands, roll them in crumbs and fry in hot lard, like doughnuts.

Chicken Pie.

Cut the chicken in pieces and parboil for three-quarters of an hour. Remove the chicken and add to the water in which it is boiled a little salt, pepper and a teacupful of milk thickened with a tablespoonful of flour. Line a deep dish with nice paste, put in the chicken and turn over it the gravy which you have prepared. Cover it with paste immediately; make a small hole in the center; ornament with strips of paste, and bake for forty-five minutes.

Boiled Fowl or Chicken.

They should be cleaned and stuffed as for roasting. A young fowl requires an hour; if tough and old, three hours. A chicken will boil in three-quarters of an hour. They may be served with oyster, caper or egg sauce.

Stewed Chicken.

Divide a chicken into pieces by the joints, and put into a stewpan, with salt, pepper, some parsley and thyme; pour in a quart of water, with a piece of butter; and when it has stewed an hour and a half, take the chickens out of the pan. If there is no gravy, put in another piece of butter, add some water and flour, and let it boil a few minutes. When done, it should not be quite as thick as drawn butter. For the dumplings: Take one quart of sifted flour, one teaspoonful of salt, two of cream of tartar and one of soda; mix with milk and form into biscuit; place them upon a tin in a steamer over the kettle where the chicken is boiling. They will steam in twenty minutes. You can rub a little butter in the flour, if you wish them very nice.

To Cook Poultry.

All kinds of poultry and meat can be cooked quicker by adding to the water in which they are boiled a little vinegar or a piece of lemon. By the use of a little acid there will be a considerable saving of fuel, as well as shortening of time. Its action is beneficial on old tough meats, rendering them quite tender and easy of digestion. Tainted meats and fowls will lose their bad taste and odor if cooked in this way, and if not used too freely no taste of it will be acquired.

Roast Rabbit.

Time, three-quarters of an hour.—Procure a fine large rabbit, and truss it in the same manner as a hare; fill the paunch with veal stuffing, and roast it before a bright clear fire for three-quarters of an hour, if a large one basting it well with butter. Before serving mix a spoonful of flour with four of milk, stir into it the yolks of two well-beaten eggs, and season with a little grated nutmeg, pepper and salt; baste the rabbit thickly with this, to form a light coating over it. When dry, baste it with butter to froth it up, and when done place it carefully in a dish, and pour round it some brown gravy boiled up with the liver minced, and a little grated nutmeg. Serve with gravy in a tureen, and red jelly.

66

To Blanch Rabbits, Fowls, etc.

To blanch or whiten a rabbit or fowl it must be placed on the fire in a small quantity of water, and let boil. As soon as it boils it must be taken out and plunged into cold water for a few minutes.

Boiled Rabbit.

Time (medium size), three-quarters of an hour.—When the rabbit is trussed for boiling, put it into a stewpan and cover it with hot water, and let it boil very gently until tender. When done place it on a dish, and smother it with onions, or with parsley and butter, or liver sauce, should the flavor of onion not be liked. If liver sauce is to be served, the liver must be boiled for ten minutes, minced very fine and added to the butter sauce. An old rabbit will require quite an hour to boil it thoroughly.

To Fricasee Rabbits Brown.

Time, three-quarters of an hour.—Take two young rabbits, cut them in small pieces, slit the head in two, season them with pepper and salt, dredge them with flour, and fry them a nice brown in fresh butter. Pour out the fat from the stewpan, and put in a pint of gravy, a bunch of sweet herbs, half a pint of fresh mushrooms, if you have them, and three shallots chopped fine; season with pepper and salt, cover them close, and let them stew for half an hour. Then skim the gravy clean, add a spoonful of catsup and the juice of half a lemon. Take out the herbs, and stir in a piece of butter rolled in flour, boil it up till thick and smooth, skim off the fat, and serve the rabbits garnished with lemon.

To Truss Woodcocks, Snipes, etc.

Pluck and wipe them very clean outside; truss them with the legs very close to the body, and the feet pressing upon thighs; skin the head and neck, and bring the beak under the wink.

CURING BACON, HAMS, ETC.—POTTING, ETC.

Great care must be taken in preparing the meat for salting. It must be carefully examined to see that it is fresh and good, then wiped, sprinkled with salt, and afterwards left to drain a few hours before it is rubbed with the salt. The meat will thus be thoroughly cleansed from the blood, which will prevent it from turning and tasting strong. It should then be placed in

67

the pickling pan and turned every morning, also it should be rubbed with the pickle. The cover of the pickling pan should fit very close and have a weight on it to keep it down. If a large quantity of salt meat is frequently required, the pickle may be boiled up, skimmed well, and when cold poured over any meat that has been sprinkled and well drained, as above directed.

To Cure Bacon.

Time, three weeks.—Take one pound of saltpetre, one pound of bay salt, one gallon of coarse salt, one pound of salprunella, one pound of moist sugar.

Pound the salprunella and bay salt very fine, mix the coarse salt and the sugar well together, and rub it into your bacon, hams, and cheeks, putting all in the same brine. Turn and rub the bacon every day for a week; afterward, every other day. Let it remain in the brine three weeks, and then send it to be smoked or dried. Large sides of bacon take a month to dry, small ones three weeks.

To Cure Hams.

For two large hams, one pound of common salt, three ounces of bay salt, two ounces of saltpetre, one pound of coarse brown sugar, one quart of stale strong beer or ale.

Boil all the above ingredients in the quart of beer or ale, and when cold pour it on the hams and turn them every day for a fortnight, then smoke them well.

To Pot Beef.

Time, three hours and a half.—Take a piece of lean beef and free it from the skin and gristle, put it into a covered jar with three dessertspoonfuls of hot water and stand it in a deep stewpan of boiling water to boil slowly for nearly four hours, taking care that the water does not reach to the top of the jar. When done, take it out, mince it fine and pound it in a mortar with a seasoning of pepper, salt and pounded mace. When smooth and like a thick paste, mix in some clarified butter, and very little of the gravy from the jar, press it into pots, pour butter over the tops, and tie down for use.

To Pickle Pork.

Take one-third of saltpetre, two-thirds of white salt. Some people prefer pork pickled with salt alone (legs especially), others in the following manner: Put a layer of salt at the bottom of a tub; then mix the salt and saltpetre beaten; cut the pork in pieces, rub it well with the salt and lay it close in the tub, with a layer of salt between every layer of pork till the tub is full. Have a cover just large enough to fit the inside of the tub, put it on, and lay a great weight at the top and as the salt melts it will keep it close. When you want to use it, take a piece out, cover the tub over again, and it will keep good a long time.

Potted Ox-Tongue.

Cut about a pound and a half from an unsmoked boiled tongue, remove the rind. Pound it in a mortar as fine as possible with six ounces of butter and a small spoonful each of mace, nutmeg, and cloves beaten fine. When perfectly pounded and the spice well blended with the meat, press it into small potting-pans and pour clarified butter over the top. A little roast veal added to the potted tongue is an improvement.

Hams, Tongues, and Beef, Yorkshire Fashion.

Take one pound and a half of ham sugar, two ounces of salt-petre, one pound of common salt, half a pound of bay salt, two ounces of pepper.

The meat should be well rubbed over night with common salt and well rubbed in the morning with the above ingredients. If hams, they should be rubbed before the fire every day and turned.

Potted Fowl and Ham.

Cut all the meat from a cold fowl and remove the bones, skin, etc., then cut it into shreds, with a quarter of a pound of lean ham and six ounces of butter, the pepper, salt, nutmeg and cayenne, and pound it all in a mortar until reduced to a smooth paste. Then mix it thoroughly together, fill the potting-pots, pour over them a thick layer of clarified butter, and tie them down with a bladder. Set them in a dry place and it will keep good for some time. A little grated lemon peel is an improvement to the fowl.

Potted Head.

Time, five or six hours.—Take half an ox-head, and soak it in salt and water. When well cleansed from the blood, put it with two cow-heels into a large stewpan and cover them with cold water. Set over the fire and let it boil till tender. Strain the meat from the liquor, and when cold, cut the meat and gristle into very small pieces. Take all the fat from the cold liquor in which the meat, etc., was first boiled, put the mince with it, and boil the whole slowly till perfectly tender and thick enough to jelly; give it a quick boil, and put it in shapes. Before boiling the second time, add pepper and salt to your taste, and a little pounded mace if approved.

Potted Herrings.

Time, two hours.—Cut off the heads and tails of the fish, clean, wash and dry them well, sprinkle them with pepper and salt within and without, lay them in an earthen pan, and cover them with white vinegar. Set them in an oven not too hot (the roes at the top, but they are not to be eaten), till the bones are quite soft, which will be in about two hours. Some cut the fish down by the bone, so as to open them, and then roll them up from the tail to the head. The bay leaves are an improvement, and a little water may be added to the vinegar if proferred. Cover them with paper.

To Pot Lobsters.

Time, three-quarters of an hour to one hour to boil the lobster.—Take from a hen lobster the spawn, coral, flesh and pickings of the head and claws, pound well and season with cayenne, white pepper and mace, according to taste. Mix it to a firm paste with good melted butter. Pound and season the flesh from the tail and put it into a pot, and then fill with the other paste. Cover the top of each put with clarified butter and keep it in a cool place.

VEGETABLES, VEGETABLE PUREES, SALADS AND SALAD MIXTURE.

Potato Croquettes.

Season cold mashed potatoes with pepper, salt and nutmeg. Beat to a cream, with a tablespoonful of melted butter to every cupful of potato. Add two or three beaten eggs and some minced parsley. Roll into small balls; dip in beaten egg, then in bread crumbs, and fry in hot lard.

Saratoga Fried Potatoes.

Peel good sized potatoes and slice them as evenly as possible. Drop them into ice water, have a kettle of very hot lard, as for cakes, put a few at a time into a towel and shake, to dry the moisture out of them and then drop them into the boiling lard. Stir them occasionally and when of a light brown take them out with a skimmer, and they will be crisp and not greasy. Sprinkle salt over them while hot.

Stewed Potatoes.

Boil the potatoes till tender; cut them in thick slices; take a half a teaspoonful of flour, a little salt and butter and chopped parsley, and a teacupful of milk; put them all together in a saucepan and let them stew about twenty minutes.

Potato Cakes.

Roast some potatoes in the oven; when done skin and pound in a mortar with a small piece of butter warmed in a little milk; chop a shallot and a little parsley very finely, mix well with the potatoes, add pepper and salt, shape into cakes, egg and bread crumb them, and fry a light brown.

To Cook Salsify.

Scrape the root and put into cold water immediately; cut into thin slices; boil tender, make a nice white sauce or drawn butter and pour over, or boil to a mash; mix with butter, salt, a little milk and pepper, add flour enough and mix as codfish cakes, and fry in the same manner.

Egg Plant au Gratin.

Peel and cut them in slices lengthwise, arrange them in layers on a well buttered tin (previously rubbed with garlic). Put between the layers a sprinkling of fine bread crumbs, chopped parsley, sweet herbs, pepper and salt to taste; pour over them some liquified butter; add a sprinkling of grated cheese and a few baked bread crumbs; bake in the oven and brown with a salamander.

To Cook Spinach.

Wash and clean the spinach thoroughly from grit, then boil it in salt and water; press the water entirely out of it and chop it as fine as powder. A quarter of an hour before serving it put it into a saucepan with a piece of butter mixed with a tablespoonful of flour and half a tumblerful of boiling water, some salt, pepper and nutmeg, and let it simmer fifteen minutes. Serve with hard-boiled eggs on the top.

Escalloped Onions.

Take eight or ten onions of good size, slice them, and boil till tender. Lay them in a baking dish, putting bread crumbs, butter in small bits, pepper and salt between each layer, until the dish is full, putting bread crumbs last; add milk or cream until full. Bake twenty minutes or half an hour.

71

Stewed Tomatoes.

Pour boiling water over the tomatoes, and remove the skins; cut them in pieces and stew them without water, seasoning them with butter and salt, and a little pepper if desired.

Tomatoes Fried.

Do not pare them, but cut in slices as an apple; dip in cracker, pounded and sifted and fry in a little good butter.

Green Corn.

Time, twenty minutes.—This should be cooked on the same day it is gathered; it loses its sweetness in a few hours, and must be artificially supplied. Strip off the husks, pick out all the silk and put it in boiling water, if not entirely fresh, add a tablespoonful of sugar to the water, but no salt; boil twenty minutes, fast, and serve; or you may cut it from the cob, put in plenty of butter and a little salt, and serve in a covered vegetable dish.

Succotash.

Time, two hours.—Cut off the corn from the cobs, and put the cobs in just enough water to cover them and boil one hour; then remove the cobs and put in the corn and stringbeans (carefully prepared by breaking off both ends and stringing) about one inch long; add a piece of salt pork and boil one hour; when boiled add some cream, or milk, salt and pepper, and butter.

Parsnip Fritters.

Time, one hour and a half to boil.—Boil four or five parsnips until tender, take off the skins and mash them very fine, add to them a teaspoonful of flour, one egg, well beaten, and a seasoning of salt. Make the mixture into small cakes with a spoon, and fry them on both sides a delicate brown in boiling butter or beef dripping; when both sides are done, serve them up very hot on a napkin or hot dish, according to your taste.

To Serve Celery.

Wash the roots free from dirt, and cut off all the decayed leaves; preserve as much of the stalk as you can, removing any specks or discolored parts. Divide it lengthwise into quarters, curl the top leaves, and place it with the roots downwards in a celery glass nearly filled with cold water.

Stewed Celery.

Time, one hour and twenty minutes.—Wash four heads of celery very clean, take off the dead leaves, and cut away any spots or discolored parts. Cut them into pieces about two or three inches long, and stew them for nearly half an hour. Then take them out with a slice, strain the water they were stewed in, and add it to half a pint of veal gravy, mixed with three or four tablespoonfuls of cream. Put in the pieces of celery and let them stew for nearly an hour longer. Serve with the sauce poured over.

To Dress Cucumbers.

Pare the cucumbers, commence cutting from the thick end, using a sharp knife and as thin as possible, drop in a large pan of cold water, wring them in the hands, squeezing out all of the seeds (which will float); skim, or pour off the seeds, and arrange on a large dish, dress with French dressing to suit taste. This receipt makes them deliciously crisp.

Rice Croquettes.

One teacupful of rice; boil in a pint of milk and a pint of water, when boiled and hot add a piece of butter the size of an egg, two tablespoonfuls of sugar, two eggs, juice and grated peel of one lemon; stir this up well, have ready the yolks of two eggs, beaten on a plate, cracker crumbs on another; make the rice in rolls and dip in the egg and crumbs; fry them in butter; serve hot.

Young Beets Boiled.

Wash them very clean, but neither scrape nor cut them. Put them in boiling water, and, according to their size, boil them from one to two hours; take off the skin when done, and put over them pepper, salt and a little butter. Beets are very nice baked, but require a much longer time to cook.

Lima Beans.

Shell them into cold water; let them lie half an hour or longer, put them into a saucepan with plenty of boiling water, a little salt, and cook until tender. Drain and butter well and pepper to taste.

Stringbeans.

Break off both ends and string carefully; if necessary, pare both edges with a knife. Cut the beans in pieces an inch long and put in cold water a few minutes. Drain and put them into boiling water with a piece of bacon or salt pork. Boil quickly for half an hour, or till tender. Drain in a colander and dish with plenty of butter.

Fried Parsnips.

Boil until tender, scrape off the skin and cut in lengthwise slices. Dredge with flour and fry in hot dripping, turning when one side is browned.

Boiled Cabbage.

Take off the outer leaves, cut the head in quarters, and boil in a large quantity of water until done. Drain and press out the water, chop fine and season. Boil three-quarters of an hour, or till tender. The water can be drained off when they are half done, and fresh water added if desired.

Boiled Onions.

Skin them and soak them in cold water an hour or longer; then put into a saucepan and cover with boiling water, well salted; when nearly done, pour off the water, add a little milk, and simmer till tender. Season with butter, pepper and salt.

Winter Squash.

Cut it in pieces, take out the seeds and pare as thin as possible; steam or boil until soft and tender. Drain and press well, then mash with butter, pepper, salt and a very little sugar. Summer squash may be cooked the same way; if extremely tender they need not be pared.

Hashed Browned Potatoes.

So frequently husbands who travel and enjoy certain dishes as served in hotels and restaurants, request their wives at home to attempt these potatoes. They are rather difficult to prepare, but a little practice will reward one with success in the effort. Chop two cold boiled potatoes fine, dust with salt and pepper; put one tablespoonful of butter in the fryingpan, and when hot add potatoes, spreading them out evenly. A quarter of a cup of milk may be added or one-eighth teaspoon of kitchen bouquet, if liked. Have only a moderate heat, let potatoes stand to cook and brown for about ten or fifteen minutes without stirring. Then fold and roll as you would an omelet, and turn on a heated dish to serve very hot.

Do not be deceived by those that tell you they can produce something from nothing—it is impossible.

The first thing is to procure "the best," and use it to the best advantage.

Don't believe that you can give a luncheon for eight persons—Cost 95 cents with a menu as follows:

Anchovy Paste and Sliced Tomatoes on Toast
Bouillon with Marrowbone Dumplings
Macaroni Italienne
Marinated Round Steak, Breaded and Fried
Fried Potatoes   Asparagus Salad
Individual Strawberry Shortcake

It is a Joke, a Dream, both as to menu and cost.

Follow your own ideas, make everything count, make the table look attractive, strive to please, and you will succeed in not only being a good housekeeper and cook, but make home happy.

SALADS.

Yolk of one or two raw eggs; one or two young onions or leeks; three tablespoonfuls of salad oil; one of vinegar; some lettuce, and slices of beetroot, salt and mustard.

Take the yolk of one or two raw eggs, according to the size of the salad you require, beat them up well, add a little salt and mustard, and chop up one or two young onions or leeks about the size of grass, then add the salad oil and the vinegar, and beat the whole up into a thick sauce. Cut in the salad, and put thin slices of beetroot at the top. Sprinkle a little salt over it, and do not stir up till the moment you use it. For a small salad three dessert spoonfuls of oil and one of vinegar will do.

Summer Salad.

Three lettuces, a good quantity of mustard and cress, some young radishes, boiled beetroot, hard-boiled eggs. Wash and carefully remove the decayed leaves from the lettuces and mustard and cress, drain them well from the water, and cut them and the radishes into small pieces, arrange them on a dish lightly with the mustard and cress mixed with them, and any of the salad mixtures you prefer poured under, not over, them. Garnish with boiled beetroot, cucumbers and hard-boiled eggs cut into slices, and some vegetable flowers. Slices of cold poultry, or flaked fish may be added to a summer salad, and are extremely good.

75

Cold Slaugh.

Shave cabbage fine, scald half-pint vinegar, mix one small teaspoonful cornstarch in two-thirds cupful of cream (or condensed milk a very little thinner), with one egg well beaten and a little salt; pour the scalded vinegar on the mixture very slowly, so as not to break the egg, then boil until thick; pour hot on the cabbage; a few capers and olives will improve the slaugh for those who are fond of such things. The above is a very nice dish to eat, either with fried or escalloped oysters.

Potato Salad.

Six cold boiled potatoes, one medium-sized onion, sliced thin into a tureen; first a layer of potato, then of onion, alternately, until the dish is full; sprinkle with pepper and salt occasionally while filling the dish; do the same on the top; put on four tablespoonfuls of sweet cream; melt one-half cup of butter or lard from fried pork, with half a pint of vinegar; when boiling hot pour over the salad and it is ready to serve.

Lobster Salad.

Take one hen lobster, lettuces, endive, mustard and cress, radishes, beetroot, cucumber, some hard-boiled eggs; pour the salad mixture into the bowl, wash and dry the lettuces and endive, and cut them fine; add them to the dressing, with the pickings from the body of the lobster and part of the meat from the shell cut into small pieces. Rub the yolks of two or three hard-boiled eggs through a sieve, and afterward the coral of the lobster, then place the salad very lightly in the bowl, and garnish it with the coral, yolks of the hard-boiled eggs, sliced beetroot, cucumber, radishes, and the pieces of lobster; place as a border hard-boiled eggs cut across, with the delicate leaves of the celery and endive between them.

Combination Crab and Shrimp Salad.

One crab and one quart of shrimps, both picked, crisp lettuce, according to the size of the salad required; mince the lettuce in a salad bowl, covering with pure olive oil, using wooden spoon; when all oil is absorbed, add the crab and shrimps, and pour over a French dressing, mix thoroughly and serve on individual plates.

Aspics.

These are meat and vegetable jellies, easily made, and makes a beautiful garnish for cold meats, salads, etc. As a binding for mixed salads it is most attractive. For instance, chicken and celery may be mixed together molded plain or in a border, using enough aspics to hold them in shape.

It looks different than plain chicken salad.—One tablespoonful chopped onion, one tablespoonful chopped carrot, one salt spoonful celery seed or a little chopped celery, one box of gelatine (two ounces), one bay leaf, one quart of water, one level teaspoonful of salt, one tablespoonful of vinegar or lemon juice, and a dash of cayenne. Cover the gelatine with a half cup of cold water to soak for a half hour. Put all the vegetables in the quart of water, bring slowly to boiling point, simmer gently ten minutes; add seasonings; stir for a moment, add the gelatine, take from the fire and strain through two thicknesses of cheese cloth; if made carefully and quickly this will be brilliant and clear; if it boils too hard or boils too long it will be clouded. Then add the white of an egg beaten, bring to boiling point, boil rapidly for a moment, stand aside to settle for five minutes and strain through flannel or cheesecloth, and put aside to cool.

Sardine Canapes.

Spread circles of toast with sardines rubbed to paste with creamed butter, seasoned with Worcestershire sauce and few grains of cayenne. Place an olive in the center of each when ready to serve.

The Chafing Dish.

At the present time every good wife should be familiar with the chafing dish, as so many easy and inexpensive dishes may be prepared at the table, and often they are more appreciated than when brought from the kitchen.

Little Pigs in Blankets.

Take one can of finest oysters, drain off the juice, wrap each oyster in a strip of the finest thin-cut bacon you can procure, using the small Japanese toothpick for a skewer; place in a chafing dish and cook until edges of oysters ruffle, serve with fine slices of toast.

Sweetbreads a-la-Bechamel.

Time, ten minutes; six persons.—One pair of sweetbreads, two tablespoonfuls of butter, two tablespoonfuls of flour, half a cup of boiling water, half a cup of milk, half a cup of mushrooms, chopped, one level teaspoonful of salt, yolks of two eggs, one salt spoonful of pepper, six tablespoonfuls of cream. Parboil and pick apart the sweetbreads, rejecting the membrane. Put the butter and flour in the chafing dish; add the milk, salt and pepper; stir until boiling; add the sweetbreads and mushrooms. Cover the dish while you beat the yolks of the eggs and cream together; add these hastily and, when smoking hot, serve.

Chicken, game or veal may be substituted for sweetbreads.

For Cooking Venison Steak in a Chafing Dish.

Have your steaks cut from the leg and about one inch thick; trim them nicely, cutting off the outside skin and all the stray bits, and lay two steaks in a chafing dish; the lamp, of course, being ready for lighting. Prepare a gravy thus: Put into a saucepan about a cupful of nice stock, small teaspoonful of salt, half teaspoonful of black pepper, a little cayenne, a few cloves and allspice, and let boil up; then stir into it a piece of butter the size of an egg, in which one-half teaspoonful or less of flour has been rubbed, and two tablespoonfuls of currant jelly. When these are dissolved pour the gravy over the steaks; light the lamp, and while the other dishes are being served the steaks will cook; serve with currant jelly; it is exceedingly palatable and digestive. Mutton is also good prepared in this manner.

78

USEFUL KITCHEN HINTS.

Time-Table for Boiling Meats and Fish.

Mutton, per pound, 15 minutes; Corned Beef, per pound, 30 minutes; Ham, per pound, 18 to 20 minutes; Turkey, per pound, 15 minutes; Chicken, per pound, 15 minutes; Tripe, per pound, 3 to 5 hours; Codfish, per pound, 6 minutes; Halibut, per pound, 15 minutes; Bass, per pound, 10 minutes; Salmon, per pound, 10 to 15 minutes; Small Fish, per pound, 6 minutes; Lobster, per pound, 30 to 40 minutes.

Proportions.

Three to four eggs to one pint of milk for custards.
One salt spoonful of salt to one quart of milk for custards.
One teaspoonful of vanilla to one quart of milk for custards.
Two ounces of gelatine to one and three-quarters quarts of liquid.
Four heaping teaspoonfuls cornstarch to one quart of milk.
Three heaping teaspoonfuls of baking powder to one quart of flour.
One teaspoonful of soda to one pint of sour milk.
One teaspoonful of soda to one pint of molasses.
One even teaspoonful of baking powder to one cup of flour.
One teaspoonful of baking powder is the equivalent of half a teaspoonful of soda, or one teaspoonful of cream of tartar.

Tables of Weights and Measures.

Four gills, one pint; two pints, one quart; four quarts, one gallon; sixteen ounces, one pound; one-half kitchen cupful, one gill; one kitchen cupful, one-half pint or two gills; four kitchen cupfuls, one quart; two cupfuls of granulated sugar or two and one-half cupfuls of powdered sugar, one pound; one heaping teaspoonful of sugar, one ounce; one cupful of butter, one-half pound; four cupfuls of flour or one heaping quart, one pound; one heaping teaspoonful butter or butter the size of an egg, two ounces or one-quarter cup; eight round teaspoonfuls of dry material or sixteen teaspoonfuls of liquid, one cupful.

TO MAKE PASTES, PASTRY, PIES, ETC.

German Paste.

Take three-quarters of a pound of fine flour, put into it half a pound of butter, the same of powdered sugar, and the peel of a lemon grated; make a hole in the middle of the flour, break in the yolks of two eggs, reserving the whites, which are to be well beaten; then mix all well together. If the eggs do not sufficiently moisten the paste, add half an eggshell of water. Mix all thoroughly, but do not handle too much. Roll out thin, and you may use it for all sorts of pastry. Before putting it into the oven, wash over pastry with the white of the beaten eggs, and shake over a little powdered sugar.

A Light Puff Paste.

Take one pound of sifted flour, one pound of fresh butter, two teaspoonfuls of cream or tartar, one teaspoonful of soda, a little water. Work one-fourth of the butter into the flour until it is like sand, measure the cream of tartar and the soda, rub it through a sieve, put it to the flour, add enough cold water to bind it, and work it smooth; dredge flour over the paste-slab or board, rub a little flour over the rolling-pin and roll the paste to about half an inch in thickness; spread over the whole surface one-third of the remaining butter, then fold it up, dredge flour over the paste-slab and rolling-pin, and roll it out again, then put another portion of the butter, and fold and roll again, and spread on the remaining butter, and fold and roll for the last time.

Very Rich Short Crust.

Break ten ounces of butter into a pound of flour dried and sifted, add a pinch of salt and two ounces of loaf sugar rolled fine. Make it into a very smooth paste as light as possible, with two well-beaten eggs and sufficient milk to moisten the paste.

Paste for Custards.

Rub six ounces of butter into half a pound of flour. Mix it well together and two beaten eggs and three tablespoonfuls of cream. Let it stand a quarter of an hour, then work it up and roll out very thin for use.

To Ice or Glaze Pastry or Sweet Dishes.

To ice pastry or any sweet dishes, break the whites of some new-laid eggs into a large soup plate, and beat them with the blade of a knife into a firm froth. When the pastry is nearly

80

done, take it from the oven, brush it well over with the beaten egg, and sift the powdered sugar over it in the above proportion. Put it again into the oven to dry or set, taking care it is not discolored; or beat the yolks of eggs and a little warm butter well together, brush the pastry over with it when nearly baked, sift pounded sugar thickly over it and put it into the oven to dry. For raised or meat pies, the yolks of eggs must be used.

Red Currant and Raspberry Tart.

Time to bake, three-quarters of an hour.—Take a pint and a half of picked red currants, three-quarters of a pint of raspberries, a quarter of a pound of moist sugar, half a pound of puff-paste. Pick the currants and raspberries from their stalks, mix them together in a pie dish with the moist sugar. Wet the edge of the dish, place a band of puff-paste round it, wet that also. Cover the top with puff-paste, pressing it round the edge with your thumbs. Cut the overhanging edge off evenly, Then scallop the edge by first chopping it in lines all round and then giving them a little twist at regular intervals with the knife. Take the edges you have cut off, flour them, roll them out, and cut them into leaves to ornament the top. Edd it over and bake it. When done, dredge it with white sugar and salamander it.

Cherry Tart.

Time to bake, thirty-five to forty minutes.—Take about one pound and a half of cherries, half a pound of short crust, moist sugar to taste. Pick the stalks from the cherries, put in a tiny cup upside down in the middle of a deep pie dish, fill round it with the fruit, and add moist sugar to taste. Lay some short crust round the edge of the dish, put on the cover as directed before, ornament the edges and bake it in a quick oven. When ready to serve, sift some loaf sugar over the top.

Gooseberry Tart.

Time to bake, about three-quarters of an hour.—Cut off the tops and tails from a quart of gooseberries, put them into a deep pie dish with five or six ounces of good moist sugar, line the edge of the dish with short crust; put on the cover, ornament the edges and top in the usual manner, and bake in a brisk oven. Serve with boiled custard or a jug of good cream.

Cranberry Tart.

Time to bake, three quarters of an hour or one hour.—Pick a quart of cranberries free from all imperfections, put a pint of water to them, and put them into a stewpan, add a pound of fine brown sugar to them and set them over the fire to stew gently until they are soft, then mash them with a silver spoon, and turn them into pie dish to become cold. Put a puff-paste round the edge of the dish, and cover it over with a crust; or make an open tart in a flat dish with paste all over the bottom of it and round the edge; put in the cranberries; lay cross bars of paste over the top and bake.

Rhubarb Tart.

Time to bake, three-quarters of an hour to one hour.—Cut the large stalks from the leaves, strip off the outside skin and cut the sticks into pieces half an inch long. Line a pie dish with paste rolled rather thicker than a crown piece, put in a layer of rhubarb, stew the sugar over it, then fill it up with the other pieces of stalks, cover it with a rich puff-paste, cut a slit in the center, trim off the edge with a knife and bake it in a quick oven. Glaze the top or strew sugar over it.

Plain Apple Tart.

Time to bake, one hour, or if small, half an hour.—Rub a pie dish over with butter, line it with short pie crust rolled thin, pare some cooking apples, cut them in small pieces, fill the pie dish with them, strew over them a cupful of fine moist sugar, three or four cloves or a little grated lemon peel, and add a few spoonfuls of water, then cover with puff-paste crust, trim off the edges with a sharp knife and cut a small slit at each end, pass a gigling iron round the pie half an inch outside the edge, and bake in a quick oven.

Open Apple Tart.

Time, to bake, in a quick oven until the paste loosens from the dish.—Peel and slice some cooking apples and stew them, putting a small cupful of water and the same of moist sugar to a quart of sliced apples, add half a nutmeg and the peel of a lemon grated, when they are tender, set them to cool. Line a shallow tin pie dish with rich pie paste or light puff-paste, put in the stewed apples half an inch deep, roll out some of the paste, wet it slightly over with the yolk of an egg beaten with a little milk, and a tablespoonful of powdered sugar, cut it in very narrow strips, and lay them in crossbars or diamonds across the tart, lay another strip round the edge, trim off the outside neatly with a sharp knife, and bake in a quick oven until the paste loosens from the dish.

82

Tartlets.

Time, fifteen to twenty minutes.—Cut as many rounds of rich puff-paste with a tin cutter as you require. Then cut an equal number, and press a smaller cutter inside them to remove the center and leave a ring. Moisten the rounds with water and place the rings on them. Put them into a moderate oven for ten or twelve minutes, and when done fill the center with any preserve of apricot, strawberry or orange marmalade. Stamp out a little of the paste rolled very thin into stars, etc. Bake them lightly, and place one on top of each tartlet. Serve them hot or cold.

Orange Tartlets.

Time to bake, fifteen to twenty minutes.—Take out the pulp from two oranges, boil the peels until quite tender, and then beat them to a paste with twice their weight of pounded loaf sugar; then add the pulp and the juice of the oranges with a piece of butter the size of a walnut, beat all these ingredients well together, line some patty-pans with rich puff-paste, lay the orange mixture in them and bake them.

Lemon Puffs.

Time, six or eight minutes to bake.—Beat and sift a pound and a quarter of loaf sugar, and mix with it the peel of two lemons grated, whisk the whites of three eggs to a firm froth, add it gradually to the sugar and lemon, and beat it all together for one hour. Make it up into any shape you please, place the puffs on oiled paper on a tin, put them in a moderate oven and bake.

Apple Tarts.

To a quart of stewed apples run through a sieve, add three eggs, half a pound of sugar, one ounce of butter, nutmeg and rosewater to taste; paste at bottom only. Half a peck of apples makes five good-sized pies.

Rhubarb Pie.

Take some fine rhubarb, strip off the skins, and cut the sticks into inch pieces; fill a large dish with them, cover with sugar and flavor with lemon juice and peel, cinnamon or vanilla. Put this in the oven and when considerably shrunk put into a smaller dish, add more sugar and flavoring if required, cover with a good crust and bake for about half an hour.

Squash Pies.

Boil and sift a good, dry squash, thin it with boiling milk until it is about the consistency of thick milk porridge. To every quart of this add three eggs, two great spoonfuls of melted butter, nutmeg (or ginger, if you prefer), and sweeten quite sweet with sugar. Bake in a deep plate with an undercrust.

Lemon Maringue Pie.

Boil three lemons until they are soft enough for a straw to penetrate the rind, mash them up fine with a tablespoonful of butter, one cup and a half of powdered sugar, and the yolks of six eggs; make a thin crust, put in the mixture and bake it; when cool, beat up the whites of the eggs with one and a half cups of powdered sugar and spread it over the pie; brown it a nice color.

Boston Cream Pie.

Cream part.—One pint of new milk, two eggs, three tablespoonfuls of sifted flour, five tablespoonfuls of sugar. Put two-thirds of the milk on to boil, and stir the sugar and flour in what is left. When the rest boils, put in the whole and stir until it cooks thoroughly. When cool, flavor with lemon or vanilla.

Crust part.—Three eggs, beaten separately, one cup of granulated sugar, one and a half cups of sifted flour, one teaspoonful of baking powder. Divide in half, put in two pie tins, and bake in a quick oven to a straw color. When taken out split in halves, and spread the cream between.

Lemon Pie.

Yolks of four eggs, and one whole one, nine tablespoonfuls of granulated sugar, juice of two lemons and the grated rind of one, three pounded milk crackers soaked in one tumbler of milk, mix and bake. Then beat the whites of the four eggs with four tablespoonfuls of powdered or fine granulated sugar, and spread and put in the oven to brown. This makes two pies.

Lemon Pie Without any Thickening but the Eggs.

Mix together the grated rind of two lemons and the juice (discarding the hard pulp), nine tablespoonfuls of white sugar, the yolks of four eggs, two tablespoonfuls of melted butter, and half a tumbler of milk; line a dinner plate with rich crust, two layers on the edge; pour the mixture in and bake; while baking beat the whites of the eggs to a stiff froth, adding two even tablespoonfuls of powdered sugar; when the pie is sufficiently

cooked, pour over the whites and return to the over for a few
minutes.

Ye Ancient Gingerbread.

One pint sorghum molasses, 1 cup (genuine) sour buttermilk, 1 cup home-made leaf lard, 1 level tablespoonful soda, ¾
tablespoon ginger, 1 teaspoon allspice, 1 tablespoon cinnamon,
¼ teaspoon salt, 2 eggs and flour to make a soft dough.

Mix lard and molasses, add beaten eggs, then add spices,
salt and soda sifted with about one cup of flour and alternate
with the milk, beating all well together. Finally add flour
enough to make a soft dough. Roll rather thick, cut in fan-
tastic shapes, "little gingerbread men," if to please the little
folks, or any desired shape. Have a moderate heat only, as
bread should not be baked too quickly.

Shortcake need not be confined exclusively to the strawberry season. Other berries and fruits and meats can be
utilized for very acceptable variety in cakes. What is known
as "biscuit dough," more or less rich was the original shortcake, and the sweet cakes with elaborate fillings are the res-
taurant, or modern departures.

A Rich Short Cake Crust.

Is made by this recipe: Sift together 1½ cups of pastry
flour, ½ cup cornstarch, ½ teaspoon salt, 1 level tablespoon
sugar, 4 level or 2 rounding teaspoons baking powder. Cut into
this with a knife or work in with finger tips, ¼ cup butter; add
white of one egg beaten stiff; then add gradually, about one
cup of milk, making a dough similar to pie crust, in that it is
flaky and not too soft. Fold and knead lightly. Divide into
two cakes, pat into rounds or squares and bake in cake tins in
moderately quick oven 15 to 20 minutes. Individual shortcakes
may be made from this dough, and they are very attractive when
served.

The preparation of berries and fruit is so largely a matter
of taste that we leave this to the discrimination of the individual, offering but few suggestions. All fruit for shortcakes
should be prepared long enough however, in advance, to have
been sweetened by allowing sugar to remain a short time on
the cut fruit. When cream that may be whipped is obtainable,
it takes first rank as being most appropriate and acceptable
for serving with shortcakes and admits of a display of taste in
garnishing. What could be more appetizing and satisfying than
a delicious strawberry shortcake, surrounded with berries, cov-

ered with whipped cream, through which the largest and choicest berries were peeping, tempting one to "come, eat and be merry."

Tomato Pie.

Take six or eight tomatoes, two lemons, one teaspoonful flour, and sugar to taste. Crust top and bottom.

Orange Pie.

Two oranges, eight tablespoonfuls of sugar, four eggs, two-thirds tumbler of milk; beat the yolks, sugar, and grated peel of the oranges, being careful not to grate off.

White Potato Pie.

For one good-sized pie, taks half a pound of potatoes, boil and mash, and while hot squeeze half a lemon into it with a good-sized piece of butter; add one cup white sugar, two or three eggs, half a teaspoonful of mace and grate nutmeg on top of pie.

Potato Pie.

Boil either Irish or sweet potatoes until well done, mash and sift them through a coarse wire sieve; to a pint of pulp add three pints of sweet milk, a tablespoonful of melted butter, two eggs, a teacupful of sugar, half a teaspoonful of salt, nutmeg or lemon to flavor. Bake it with an undercrust of rich paste.

Apple Pie.

Stew a dozen tart apples, when soft add a tablespoonful of butter, one cup of sugar, half a glass of rosewater, and a little nutmeg. Bake the paste as for cream pie, and fill with apple instead of cream.

Auntie's Cream Pies.

Make the paste for three pies, roll out and cover your plates, then roll out and cover a second time, and bake. When baked, and while warm, separate the edges with a knife and lift the upper from the lower paste; fill in the cream, and put on the upper paste.

The Cream.—Put on a pint of milk to boil. Break two eggs into a dish, and add one cup of sugar and half a cup of flour; after beating well, stir it into the milk just as it commences to boil; keep on stirring one way until it thickens; use any flavor you may prefer.

86

Baked Apple Dumplings.

Make a crust as for soda biscuit, peel and core your apples, cut the dough in square pieces, and put one apple for each dumpling; put them in a dripping pan and place in the oven for five minutes, then make a syrup with water and sugar, one cupful of sugar to a pint of water, and pour into the dripping pan, baste with the syrup (as you would a turkey), while they are cooking; when done, eat with sweet cream.

MINCE MEAT.

One pound of currants, one pound of peeled and chopped apples, one pound of suet chopped fine, one pound of moist sugar, quarter of a pound of raisins stoned and cut in two, the juice of four oranges and two lemons, with the chopped peel of one; add of ground mace and allspice each a spoonful, and a wineglass of brandy. Mix all well together and keep it closely covered in a cool place.

Egg Mince Meat.

Six hard-boiled eggs, shred very fine; double the quantity of beef suet, chopped very small; one pound of currants, washed and dried; the peel of one large or two small lemons, minced up; six tablespoonfuls of sweet wine, a little mace, nutmeg and salt, with sugar to your taste; add a quarter of a pound of candied orange and citron cut into thin slices. Mix all well together and press it into a jar for use.

Lemon Mince Meat.

Take one large lemon, three large apples, four ounces of beef suet, half a pound of currants, four ounces of white sugar, one ounce of candied orange and citron. Chop up the apples and beef suet; mix them with the currants and sugar; then squeeze the juice from a large lemon into a cup. Boil the lemon thus squeezed till tender enough to beat to a mash; add it to the mince meat. Pour over it the juice of the lemon, and add the citron chopped fine.

BAKED AND BOILED PUDDINGS.

For boiled puddings you will require either a mould, a basin, or a pudding cloth; the former should have a close-fitting cover and be rubbed over the inside with butter before putting the pudding in it, that it may not stick to the side; the cloth should be dipped in boiling water, and then well floured on the inside. A pudding cloth must be kept very clean, and in a dry place. Bread puddings should be tied very loosely, as they swell very much in boiling.

The water must be boiling when the pudding is put in, and continue to boil until it is done. If a pudding is boiled in a cloth it must be moved frequently while boiling, otherwise it will stick to the sauce pan.

There must always be enough water to cover the pudding if it is boiled in a cloth; but if boiled in a tin mould do not let the water quite reach the top.

To boil a pudding in a basin, dip a cloth in hot water, dredge it with flour and tie it closely over the basin. When the pudding is done, take it from the water, plunge whatever it is boiling in, whether cloth or basin, suddenly into cold water, then turn it out immediately; this will prevent its sticking. If there is any delay in serving the pudding, cover it with a napkin or the cloth in which it was boiled; but it is better to serve it as soon as removed from the cloth, basin or mould.

Always leave a little space in the pudding basin for the pudding to swell, or tie the pudding cloth loosely for the same reason.

Baked Puddings.

Bread or rice puddings require a moderate heat for baking; batter or custard require a quick oven.

Eggs for puddings are beaten enough when a spoonful can be taken up clear from the strings.

Souffles require a quick oven. These should be made so as to be done the moment for serving, otherwise they will fall in and flatten.

Noodle Pudding.

Time, one hour.—Three eggs, beat light; add a little salt and flour to make a paste that will roll; roll the paste an eighth of an inch thick; fold the paste and shred fine; boil in clear water, with a little salt, put them in the water while it is boiling, and do not allow them to stick together, or uncover the pot for ten minutes; take them out and drain well; bake them one hour; beat two eggs light, mix them in a quart of milk, and stir in the noodles; add salt, sugar and spices to taste, and bake as custard.

Yankee Plum Pudding.

Time, four hours.—Take a tin pudding boiler that shuts over tight with a cover. Butter it well. Put at the bottom some stoned raisins and then a layer of baker's bread, cut in slices, with a little butter or suet strewed over, then raisins, bread and suet alternately, until you nearly fill the tin. Take milk enough to fill your boiler, and to every quart add three or four eggs, some nutmeg and salt, and sweeten with half sugar and half molasses. Drop it into boiling water, and let it boil three or four hours. Be sure the cover fits tight, or your pudding will be watersoaked. Serve with wine sauce.

John Bull Pudding.

Time, six hours.—One pound of flour, one pound stoned raisins, one pound currants, quarter of a pound sugar, one ounce citron, one pound suet chopped fine, six eggs beaten very light, one gill good brandy. Some of the flour (sifted) should be reserved to mix with the dry fruit. Boil six hours; keep boiling water at hand to replenish as it boils; to be eaten with hard or liquid sauce, as taste may dictate; turn the pudding a few times when you first put it to boil.

Cheap Plum Pudding.

Time, three hours.—One cup suet, one cup raisins, one cup currants and citron mixed, one egg, one cup sweet milk, half a teacup molasses, one teaspoonful soda, three and a half cups flour, a little salt; boil three hours; serve with hard or liquid sauce.

Plum Pudding.

Time, three hours.—A pint of bread crumbs; pour over them one-half pint boiling milk and let it cool thoroughly; then add one pound stoned raisins, one-half pound currants, one tablespoonful of butter minced fine, one tablespoonful of flour, one tablespoonful of sugar, one small teaspoonful cloves, nutmeg and cinnamon, each; five eggs, beaten light; flour your fruit before mixing, and boil three hours; eat with hot brandy sauce.

Indian Pudding.

Time, two hours.—Scald one pound of Indian meal—that is, pour boiling water on it, stirring until stiff; have ready one pound chopped suet; stir it in and add one pint molasses and one ounce ground ginger; bake in a greased tin in a slow oven; takes about two hours to bake.

Troy Pudding.

Time, three hours.—One cup each of chopped suet, stoned raisins, molasses and milk, and one egg, three cups of sifted flour, a little salt and a pinch of soda; boil three hours; serve with sweet sauce.

Poor Man's Pudding.

Time, two hours.—Into two quarts of boiling water stir six heaping tablespoonfuls of meal, a little salt and a piece of butter the size of an egg. When nearly cold add three well-beaten eggs and eight tablespoonfuls of sugar or molasses and spice to taste.

Orleans Pudding.

Time, two hours.—Two cups flour, one-half cup butter, one cup molasses, one cup raisins, one and a half cups of milk, one teaspoonful saleratus dissolved in milk; boil two hours in tin boiler; serve with the above sauce.

Boiled Fruit Pudding.

Time, two hours.—One quart crushed wheat, one teaspoonful cinnamon, half teaspoonful cloves, two cups sugar, two eggs, half a pound of suet, chopped fine, one teaspoonful cream of tartar, half a teaspoonful of soda, half cup of molasses, half pound of raisins chopped fine, citron or lemon peel if desired; boil two hours.

Orange Pudding.

Time, twenty minutes.—Four sweet oranges peeled and picked to pieces, and put in a deep pudding dish, with two cups of sugar. Put a quart of milk, the yolks of three eggs and two dessert spoonfuls of cornstarch on to boil; take off, cool it, and pour it on the oranges; then beat the whites to a stiff froth, put it over the pudding, and place it in the oven until it is of a light brown color.

Farina Pudding.

Time, three-quarters of an hour.—Five ounces farina stirred gradually and boiled in one quart of milk, then let it cool, separate the yolks and whites of five eggs, beat the whites to a stiff froth, and stir the yolks and sugar together, then stir all into the cool boiled farina, flavor and bake; it will be light like a souffle if made in this manner.

90

Queen Pudding.

Time, half an hour.—One quart milk, one pint (hardly full) bread crumbs, four eggs—yolks, whites for frosting, sugar to taste. Serve with hard sauce and jelly; when the pudding is done pour over it the whites of the eggs and brown.

Two-Hour Pudding.

One-half cup butter, one-half cup sugar, one-half cup (small) molasses, one cup milk, two cups flour, one and a quarter cups raisins, hard sauce; grease the tin well with butter, and let it boil two hours.

Apple Pudding.

Time, two hours.—Peel the apples and put them in a kettle in halves, with a pint of water, a small lump of butter, a little salt, nutmeg, and a handful of sugar, make a soda biscuit crust about one-third inch thick, and put it on top of the apples, make a hole in the center of the crust, boil until the apples are thoroughly cooked. Serve with hot sauce, adding wine or brandy if you choose. A plate turned upside down in the kettle will prevent it from burning.

French Tapioca Pudding.

Time, one hour.—Take two ounces of tapioca, and boil it in a half pint of water, until it begins to melt, then add half a pint of milk by degrees, and boil until the tapioca becomes very thick; add a well-beaten egg, sugar and flavoring to taste, and bake gently for three-quarters of an hour.

Bread Pudding.

Time, one hour.—Soak the bread in cold water, then squeeze it very dry, take out the lumps and add boiling milk, about a pint to a pound of soaked bread, beat up two eggs, sweeten, add a little nutmeg, and bake the pudding slowly until firm. If desired a few raisins may be added.

Aunt Mary's Pudding.

Time, two hours.—Butter a tart dish, sprinkle the bottom with finely minced candied peel, and a very little shred suet, then a thin layer of light bread, and so on until the dish is full. For a pint dish make a liquid custard of one egg and half a pint of milk; sweeten, pour over pudding, and bake as slowly as possble for two hours.

91

Children's Pudding.

Time, one hour and a half.—To make a nice pudding for the children's diner, take three eggs, three tablespoonfuls of flour, one quart of milk and a little salt; make a batter, then have some apples nicely peeled and cored, place them in a well buttered pie dish, then pour the batter over them. Let it bake one hour and half and make a nice sweet sauce for it.

Oatmeal Pudding.

Time, one hour.—Mix two ounces of fine Scotch oatmeal in a quarter of a pint of milk add to it a pint of boiling milk, sweeten to taste and stir over the fire for ten minutes; then put in two ounces of sifted bread crumbs; stir until the mixture is stiff, then add one ounce of shreded suet, and one or two well beaten eggs; add a little lemon flavoring or grated nutmeg. Put the pudding into a buttered dish and bake slowly for an hour.

Macroon Pudding.

Time, half an hour.—Soak a pound of fresh macroons in milk, make a custard of eight eggs (reserving the whites of four), a quart of milk sweetened with one-quarter pound of sugar, put the macroons in the custard, bake in a deep dish in the oven, putting a piece of paper on top to prevent burning; when done whip the whites of the four eggs, with sugar, and spread on top quite thickly, put in the oven again for about five minutes.

Hard Times Pudding.

Time, three hours.—Half a pint of molasses, half a pint of water, two teaspoonfuls of soda, one teaspoonful of salt; thicken with flour, sifted, to a batter, thick as cup cake, put into pudding boiler, half full, to allow for swelling; boil steadily for three hours; eat with or without sauce.

Pumpkin Pudding.

Time, two hours.—Pare the pumpkin and put it down to stew, strain it through a colander; two pounds of pumpkin to one pound of butter, one pound of sugar, and eight eggs; beat to a froth; one wineglass of brandy, half wineglass of rosewater, one teaspoonful mace, cinnamon and nutmeg all together.

Cornstarch Pudding.

Time, half an hour.—Boil one quart of milk, then beat the yolks of four eggs, with four tablespoonfuls of cornstarch and

92

a little milk; stir into the boiling milk, let it boil up once and turn into a pudding dish; then beat the whites of the eggs to a froth and add four spoonfuls of white powdered sugar; cover the pudding with the mixture, and set in the oven and brown lightly; flavor with vanilla, lemon, etc.

Apple Batter Pudding.

Time, one hour.—Core and peel eight apples, put in a dish, fill the places from which the cores have been taken with brown sugar, cover and bake; beat the yolks of four eggs light, add two teacupfuls of flour, with three even teaspoonfuls of baking powder, sifted with it, one pint of milk, and a teaspoonful of salt, then the whites, well beaten; pour over the apples and bake; use sauce with it.

Batter Pudding.

One quart of milk, four eggs, six spoonfuls of flour, a little sale; bake twenty minutes.

Cocoanut Pudding.

Grate cocoanut, then stew it slowly in one quart of milk; pour this on a half loaf of baker's bread; when cold add one pound of sugar, and one-half pound butter, beaten to a cream; then add six eggs and bake.

Snow Pudding.

One ounce of gelatine; pour on it a pint and a half of boiling water; add two teacups of white sugar, the grated peel and juice of two lemons; strain into a deep dish to cool; when it commences to jell, add to it the whites of four well-beaten eggs, beat until the dish is full, put in molds and place in a cool place.

Fig Pudding.

Time, four hours.—Half a pound bread crumbs, half a pound figs, six ounces of suet, six ounces brown sugar; mince the figs and suet nicely, a little salt, two eggs, well beaten, nutmeg to taste, boil in a mold four fours. Serve with wine sauce.

Mock Plum Pudding.

Time, three hours.—One cup finely cut suet, one of dried currants, one-third cup of molasses, two-thirds cup of milk or water, one teaspoonful allspice, cloves and cinnamon mixed, three cups of flour: mix well and steam three hours.

PANCAKES, FRITTERS, ETC.

Pancakes should be eaten hot. They should be light enough to toss over in the pan. Snow will serve instead of eggs for pancakes; it should be taken when just fallen, and quite clean; two tablespoonfuls of snow will supply the place of one egg.

Common Pancakes.

Time, five minutes.—Beat three eggs, and stir them into a pint of milk; add a pinch of salt, and sufficient flour to make it into a thick, smooth batter; fry them in boiling fat, roll them over on each side, drain and serve them very hot, with lemon and sugar.

Snow Pancakes.

Time, five minutes.—Make a stiff batter with four ounces of flour, a quarter of a pint of milk, or more if required, a little grated nutmeg, and a pinch of salt. Divide the batter into any number of pancakes, and add three large spoonfuls of snow to each; fry them lightly, in very good butter, and serve quickly.

Batter for Fritters.

Time, five minutes.—Mix eight ounces of fine flour with about half a pint of water into a smooth batter, dissolve the butter over a slow fire; and then stir it by degrees into the flour; then add the whites of two eggs whisked to a stiff froth, and stir them lightly in.

Apple Fritters.

Time, six minutes.—Beat and strain the yolks of seven eggs and the whites of three; mix into them a pint of new milk, a little grated nutmeg, a pinch of salt, and a glass of brandy; well beat the mixture, and then add gradually sufficient flour to make a thick batter; pare and core six large apples, cut them in slices about a quarter of an inch thick, sprinkle pounded sugar over them, and set them by for an hour or more; dip each piece of apple in the batter, and fry them in hot lard about six minutes, the lard should not be made too hot at first, but must become hotter as they are frying; serve on a napkin with sifted sugar over them.

Cake Fritters.

Cut a stale cake into slices an inch and a half in thickness, pour over them a little good cream, and fry them lightly in

94

fresh butter, and when done place over each slice of cake a layer of preserves.

Bread Fritters.

To a quart basinful of stale bread broken small, put a quart of boiling milk, cover it for ten or fifteen minutes; when quite soft, beat it with a spoon until it is smooth, add two well-beaten eggs, half a nutmeg grated, a tablespoonful of brandy, one of butter and a little salt; beat it light; make an omelet-pan hot, put in a small piece of butter and when dissolved pour in sufficient batter to run over the pan, let it fry gently; when one side is a fine brown, turn the other, put butter and sugar with a little grated nutmeg over, lay one on the. other, cut them through in quarters, and serve them hot.

Blackberry Fritters.

Time, five minutes.—Are made by mixing a thick batter of flour and sour milk, or cream as for pancakes, only quite stiff; if cream is used, allow one more egg than for sour milk, then stir thick with berries; have ready a kettle of hot lard, dip a tablespoon into the lard, then take a spoonful of batter and drop it into the boiling lard; the grease will prevent the batter from sticking to the spoon and will let it drop off in nice oval shape; eat with syrup.

Grandma's Crullers.

Time, five minutes.—Six eggs, six tablespoonfuls powdered sugar, six tablespoonfuls melted butter, a wineglass of brandy, and a little nutmeg; flour as for doughnuts; roll thin and cut into fanciful shapes with a jagging iron.

Doughnuts.

Time, five minutes.—Half a pint of sweet milk, half a cup of butter (scant), one cup.of yeast, salt; flavor with nutmeg or cinnamon; mix them at night; in the morning roll out and let them raise until very light, and drop in hot fat; they are very nice, after they are fried, to roll them in pulveried sugar.

Doughnuts.

Dissolve one cake of compressed yeast in one pint of lukewarm milk; add flour to make a moderately stiff sponge, and let rise until it begins to drop or go back (say about two hours); rub together one-quarter pound butter, one-half pound sugar, three eggs, a little extract of lemon, a little cinnamon; add

95

the same with a cup of warm milk to the sponge, an
dough as soft as it can be handled; let rise about an l
until light, then roll out, cut with round cutter, place (
dusted table until light, and then fry in hot lard.

Graham Griddle Cakes.

Time, five minutes.—One pint of milk, half a cup
cream, half a teaspoonful of soda, the same of salt;
graham flour not as stiff as for fine flour cakes (no eggs
the griddle quite hot; or with yeast the same as wit
wheat.

Hominy Croquettes.

Time, six minutes.—To a cupful of cold boiled hom
a teaspoonful melted butter, and stir it well, adding by
a cupful of milk, till all is made into a soft, light pas
a teaspoonful white sugar, and one well-beaten egg;
into oval balls with floured hands, dip in beaten eg
rolled cracker crumbs, and fry in hot lard.

Fried Bread.

Beat four eggs very light, add three tablespoonfuls
brown sugar, a little grated nutmeg, a tablespoonful of
or rosewater, and a quart of milk; cut into nice slices,
thick, a stale loaf of bread; remove the crust from th
and cut each slice into halves; butter your frying-pan, an
hot lay in your bread (dipped in the custard) and br
both sides; lay them on a hot dish and sprinkle over
little loaf sugar.

Hominy Fritters.

Two teacupfuls of cold boiled hominy, add to it c
cupful of sweet milk and a little salt, stir till smooth, tl
four tablespoonfuls of flour and one egg; beat the y
white, adding the white last; have ready a pan with ho
and lard (half of each), drop the batter in by spoonf
fry a light brown.

Omelet Souffle.

Separate the whites from the yolks of twelve eggs;
whites into a basin and beat them extremely fast till th
a very thick snow; then beat six yolks separately, w
ounces of sugar, and a dessert spoonful of orange flower
or just enough to flavor it to your taste.

Before beating the eggs have ready a round tin, well
all over the inside with fresh butter.

96

When you have finished beating the six yolks, mix them very thickly with the whites, lest the snow should turn—that is, melt into water; put it then into the buttered tin, and place it in the oven; it will be so thick, if it is well and skillfully mixed, that there will be no fear of its running over; watch it well, glancing at it from time to time through a little opening of the oven door, to see how it is going on; as soon as it has risen very high, and is of a golden color, take it out of the oven.

Do not suffer the omelet souffle to remain long in the oven; if it is not watched it will fall in and become a mere galette; let the oven be of a very gentle heat, or the bottom of the omelet will be burned before the top is done.

Before putting the tin in the oven you may powder the snow with fine sugar; it crystallizes and has a very pretty effect; as soon as the omelet is done it must be sent to the table; if it waits for longer than ten minutes it falls in; the eggs should be beaten with a fork or a little whisk.

If this souffle is liked more solid, add to the yolks of the eggs when beaten two dessert spoonfuls of rice boiled in milk and flavored with vanila; in this case do not put in the orange flower flavoring; the rice must be very well cooked, and well sweetened before it is added to the eggs.

Friar's Omelet.

Boil eight or nine large apples to a pulp, stir in two ounces of butter, and add pounded sugar to taste; when cold add an egg well beaten up; then butter the bottom of a deep baking dish, and the sides also; thickly strew crumbs of bread, so as to stick all over the bottom and sides; put in the mixture and strew bread crumbs plentifully over the top; put it into a moderate oven, and when baked turn it out, and put powdered sugar over it.

Orange Souffle.

Slice five oranges, and pour over them a cold custard made of one pint of milk, the yolks of five eggs, sweetened to taste; beat the whites of eggs to a froth, and brown carefully.

DAINTY DESSERTS FOR DAINTY PEOPLE.

Lemon Custard.

Take half a pound of loaf sugar, the juice of two lemons, the peel of one pared very thin, boiled tender and rubbed through a sieve, and a pint of white wine; let all boil for a quarter of an hour, then take out the peel and a little of the liquor and set them to cool; pour the rest into the dish you intend for it; beat the yolks of the eggs and the whites and mix them with the cool liquor; strain them into your dish, stir them well up together, and set them on a slow fire in boiling water; when done, grate the peel of a lemon on the top, and brown it over with a salamander; this custard may be eaten either hot or cold.

Plain Boiled Custard.

Time, about twenty minutes to infuse the peel, ten or fifteen minutes to stir the custard.—Pour a quart of milk into a delicately clean saucepan with three laurel leaves and the peel of a lemon, set it by the side of the fire for about twenty minutes, and when on the point of boiling strain it into a basin to cool; then stir in a quarter of a pound of loaf sugar, and the ten eggs well beaten, again strain it into a jug, which place in a deep saucepan of boiling water, and stir it one way until it thickens; then pour it into a glass dish or into custard cups.

Blancmange.

Time, fifteen minutes.—Put into a delicately clean stewpan one ounce isinglass or gelatine, two ounces of sweet and bitter almonds blanched and pounded, one pint and a half of new milk, and pint of cream, the lemon juice and the peel grated, with loaf sugar to taste; set the stewpan over a clear fire, and stir it till the isinglass is dissolved, then take it off and continue stirring it till nearly cold before putting it into the mold; this quantity will fill a quart mold, but if you wish to make it in a small shape you must not put more than a pint of milk and half a pint of cream; color the top ornament with cochineal, and let it get cold before you add the rest of the blanchmange.

Cheap Blancmange.

Time, fifteen minutes altogether.—Pour two spoonfuls of boiling water over an ounce of isinglass, take a quarter of a pound of sugar, rub part of it on the lemon, and when the flavor and color are well extracted, put it with the remainder of the sugar into a stewpan with a quart of milk and a stick of cinnamon; let it all simmer until the sugar and isinglass are dissolved; then strain it through muslin into a jug, add the vanilla flavoring, strain it again, and then pour it into a china mold and let it stand all night in a very cold place.

Milan Souffle.

Take four lemons, rub the peel on the sugar, put to it the yolks of six eggs made into a custard and the juice of the lemons; let it stand till cold, then add nearly half a pint of whipped cream and an ounce of isinglass; the whites of the eggs to be well whipped to a strong froth, and put round it with the whipped cream when cold.

New Jersey Blanchange.

In three pints of sweetened cream, or milk, put one ounce of Russia isinglass and a little salt; place it over the fire and stir in the isinglass until dissolved; then boil it well; it will not taste so rich if only scalded; flavor and strain into a pitcher, stand the pitcher where it will keep hot and all the sediment will settle; pour carefully into forms that the sediment may not darken the ornaments; if peach water or almond is used for flavoring, put it in after boiling; the peel of a lemon and stick cinnamon boiled together in milk is very pleasant.

CREAMS.

Stone Cream.

One pot of preserved apricots or plums, half an ounce of isinglass, one pint of cream, one lemon, two teaspoonfuls of crushed white sugar (more or less, to taste); take a glass dish and line it at the bottom about an inch thick with preserved plums or jam; dissolve half an ounce of isinglass in a little water, strain it, add to it a pint of thick cream, the peel of the lemon grated, enough sugar to make it pleasant to your taste; let it boil one minute, then put it into a jug that has a spout; when it is nearly cold but not quite set, squeeze into it the juice of the lemon (or rather, squeeze the lemon in a cup and add it to the cream, lest a pip should fall into the jug); pour it into the dish from a jug with a spout over the sweetmeat, and let it stand all night; place on the top a few ratafias.

Velvet Cream.

Put one ounce of isinglass into a stewpan with a large cupful of white wine, the juice of a large lemon, and sufficient sugar to sweeten it rubbed on the peel to extract the color and flavor; stir it over the fire until the isinglass is dissolved, and then strain it to get cold; then mix with it the cream and pour into a mold.

Coffee Cream.

Put three-quarters of a pint of boiled milk into a stewpan, with a large cupful of made coffee, and add the yolks of eight

99

well-beaten eggs and four ounces of pounded loaf sugar; stir the whole briskly over a clear fire until it begins to thicken, take it off the fire, stir it for a minute or two longer and strain it through a sieve on the two ounces of gelatine; mix it thoroughly together and when the gelatine is dissolved, pour the cream into a mold, previously dipped into cold water, and set the mold on rough ice to set.

Lemon Cream.

Pare into a pint of water the peels of three large lemons; let it stand four or five hours; then take them out and put to the water the juice of four lemons and six ounces of fine loaf sugar; beat the whites of six eggs and mix it all together, strain it through a lawn sieve, set it over a slow fire, stir it one way until as thick as good cream; then take it off the fire and stir it until cold, and put it into a glass dish. Orange cream may be made in the same way, adding the yolks of three eggs.

Raspberry Cream Without Cream.

Pound and sift a quarter of a pound of sugar, mix with it a quarter of a pound of raspberry jam or jelly, and the whites of four eggs; all to be beaten together for one hour, and then put in lumps in a glass dish.

Bavarian Cream.

Dissolve half a package of gelatine in one quart of boiling milk; stir until it is dissolved, then add a pint of cream, and sweeten to taste; add three tablespoonfuls of extract of vanilla; let it cool a little, stirring it occasionally; then put it into custard cups, or in a mold, and leave it in a cold place till ready to use.

American Cream.

One quart of milk, four eggs, half a box of gelatine, one and a half teaspoonfuls of vanilla; soak the gelatine in a little cold water twenty minutes; beat the yolks of the eggs and the sugar together, let the milk come to a boil, then stir in the sugar and the yolks, then the gelatine, then the whites of the eggs (having been beaten to a foam); gently stir all together, add the flavoring, and pour into a mold to cool.

JELLIES, SWEET DISHES, RELISHES, ETC.

The Foundation of all Jelly.

Take a packet of gelatine, dissolve it in half a pint of cold water, and then add a pint of hot water, the peel of five lemons

100

without the pith, a small stick of cinnamon, the cloves, the juice of the lemons, the sherry and the loaf sugar; when done clarify it with the shells and whites of five eggs.

If you wish to make any other kind of jelly, omit the sherry and add for instance, orange juice for orange jelly, or the juice of strawberries, cherries, pineapple, or any other fruit; the jelly takes its name from its flavoring; no jelly of several colors should be set warm, as the different colors run and weaken it extremely.

Calves' Feet Jelly.

Time, to boil the feet until reduced to one quart; to reboil the jelly, a quarter of an hour.—Cut two feet in small pieces after they have been well cleaned and the hair taken off; stew them very gently in two quarts of water till it is reduced to one quart; when cold take off the fat and remove the jelly from the sediment; put it into a saucepan with half a pound of loaf sugar, a pint of white wine, a wineglass of brandy in it, four lemons with the peel rubbed on the sugar, the whites of four eggs well beaten and their shells broken; put the saucepan on the fire, but do not stir the jelly after it begins to warm; let it boil a quarter of an hour after it rises to a head, then cover it close, and let it stand about half an hour; after which pour it through a jelly bag, first dipping the bag in hot water to prevent waste, and squeezing it quite dry; pour the jelly through until clear. then put it into the mold.

Jelly From Cow Heels.

Time, to boil the cowheels seven hours, or until reduced to three pints; boil five minutes after the wine is added.—Put two thoroughly clean cowheels into a stewpan with a gallon of spring water, and let it boil until reduced to three pints; when cold skim off the cake of fat and take the jelly carefully from the sediment at the bottom, put the jelly into a stewpan with one pint of white wine, half a pound of loaf sugar, and the juice of five lemons; beat up the whites of six eggs, throw them into the jelly, stir it all together, and let it boil five minutes; then pour it into a jelly bag and let it run on the peels of four lemons placed in the basin the jelly runs into; as the peel will give a fine flavor and color; if not perfectly clear, run it through again; pour into a mold, and turn it out the next day.

Apple Jelly.

Take some ripe apples, fine-flavored and juicy, pare and cut them in quarters, put them in water as you cut them, or they will turn black; when all are cut put them in a preserving kettle, and pour over them a little water; let them cook until they are quite soft, then strain through a flannel bag; boil the juice with an equal weight of sugar until it will jell (you can test it by placing a little on a plate), and pour it, while hot, into the jelly molds or jars. Golden pippin apples make the finest jelly; if wanted for immediate use only you can use less sugar.

Currant Jelly.

Mash the currants well to expel the juice; strain through a cloth, and to every pint of juice allow a pound of sugar; put the sugar in the preserving pan and add a very little water; heat gradually and boil it ten minutes, stirring constantly; skim the sugar and add the currant juice; let the sugar and currant juice cook ten minutes after they begin to boil; skim well and pour at once into glasses or jars.

Grape Jelly.

Take grapes before they are fully ripe and boil them gently with a very little water; then strain and proceed as with currant jelly. Wild grapes will not make as firm a jelly as cultivated ones.

Wine Jelly.

To one and a half boxes gelatine, one pint cold water, juice of three lemons, grated rind of two; let stand an hour, then add two pounds of loaf sugar, three pints boiling water; boil five minutes; just before straining in flannel bag stir in one pint sherry wine, six tablespoonfuls of best brandy.

Swedish Jelly.

Cover a knuckle of veal with water, add a small onion and a carrot, and let it boil until the meat is ready to fall off the bone; take the meat, hash it fine and return it to the liquor after it is strained, and give it another boil until it jellies; add salt, pepper, the juice and rind of a lemon cut fine, then pour it into a form; put it in a cold place. It makes a nice dish for lunch or tea. If the knuckle of veal is large, use three quarts of water; if small, two quarts, and let it boil slowly three or four hours, or until it is reduced to about half the quantity of water put in.

Gelatine Jelly.

To make two quarts, take a two-ounce package of the gelatine and soak for one hour in a pint of cold water, add to this one pound and a half of sugar, the juice of four lemons, some orange peel, stick cinnamon or other flavoring; when the gelatine is thoroughly soaked pour on three pints of boiling water and strain immediately through a jelly bag or coarse toweling; next pour into molds and set aside to cool; in warm weather use a little more gelatine.

Gateau de Pommes.

Boil one pound of sugar in a pint of water until the water has evaporated, then add two pounds of apples pared and cored, the juice of a large lemon, and the peel grated; boil all together till quite stiff, then put it into a mold and when cold turn it out and serve it with rich custard around it.

Gooseberry Fool.

Put two quarts of gooseberries in a stewpan with a quart of water; when they begin to turn yellow and swell, drain the water from them and press them with the back of a spoon through a colander, sweeten them to your taste, and set them to cool; put two quarts of milk over the fire beaten up with the yolks of four eggs and a little grated nutmeg; stir it over the fire until it begins to simmer, then take it off and stir it gradually into the cold gooseberries; let it stand until cold and serve it. The eggs may be left out and milk only may be used. Half this quantity makes a good dishful.

Rice Snow Balls.

Time, twenty minutes to boil the rice.—Put a quarter of a pound of rice into a stewpan with a pint and a half of new milk, two ounces of pounded sugar and two ounces of sweet almonds blanched and minced fine, and boil it until the rice is tender; dip some small cups into cold water, fill them with the rice and set them to become cold; turn them out on a dish, arrange a border of preserves or marmalade all round them, and pour a little rich cream into the center, if you have it.

Frosted Pippins.

Time, half an hour.—Divide twelve pippins, take out the cores, and place them close together on a tin, with the flat side downward. Whisk the white of egg quite firm, spread it over them, then strew some lemon peel cut very thin and in shreds, and sift double refined sugar over the whole. Bake them half an hour, and then place them on a hot dish and serve them quickly.

103

Rice and Pears.

Time, one hour and a half.—Boil a cup and a half of rice in one pint of milk till tender, then put in the cinnamon, sugar and nutmeg. Take it up, let it get nearly cold, beat three eggs well, and mix them with the rice; butter a mold, put the rice in, tie it down tightly in a floured cloth, and let it boil for an hour; turn it out, lay round it baked pears. Garnish with slices of lemon stuck into the rice.

Meringues.

Whisk the whites of four small eggs to a high froth, then stir into it half a pound of finely powdered sugar; flavor it with vanilla, or lemon essence, and repeat the whisking until it will lie in a heap; then lay the mixture in lumps on letter paper, in the shape of half an egg, molding it with a spoon, laying each about half an inch apart; then place the paper containing the meringues on a piece of hard wood, and put them into a quick oven; do not close it; watch them, and when they begin to have a yellow appearance take them out; remove the paper carefully from the wood, and let them cool for two or three minutes; then slip a thin-bladed knife very carefully under one, turn it into your left hand, take another from the paper in the same way, and join the two sides which were next the paper together. The soft inside may be taken out with the handle of a small spoon, the shells filled with jam, jelly, or cream and then joined together as above, cementing them together with some of the mixture.

Rice Meringue.

Time, twenty minutes.—Put a teacupful of rice into half a pint of milk, and stand it at the side of the fire to simmer until quite soft; then add the yolks of three beaten eggs to the rice in the stewpan, and beat the whole up with a teaspoonful of fine, moist sugar; then turn it out into the tin that it is to be baked in, piling it up high in the center, and spread a thick layer of apricot or any other jam over it; whisk the whites of the three eggs to a firm froth with a teaspoonful of powdered loaf sugar, spread it all over the jam and sprinkle loaf sugar on the top of it; then drop a little of the froth about it in different shapes; put it into the oven for about twenty minutes, leaving the door open. Raspberry, strawberry or currant jam may be used.

Curd for Cheesecakes.

Boil one quart of water in a stewpan; beat two eggs and mix them with a quart of new milk; then add them to the water, with two spoonfuls of lemon juice of good vinegar; when the curd rises lay it on a sieve to drain.

Cheesecakes.

Time, fifteen to twenty minutes.—Beat half a pint of good curd with four eggs, three spoonfuls of rich cream, a quarter of a nutmeg grated, a spoonful of ratafia, and a quarter of a pound of currants washed and dried; mix all well together and bake in patty-pans lined with a good puff-paste.

Lemon Cheesecakes.

Time, fifteen to twenty minutes.—Just warm a quarter of a pound of butter, stir into it a quarter of a pound of sugar pounded fine, and when dissolved mix with it the peel of two lemons grated and the juice of one strained; mix all well together, and pour it into patty-pans lined with puff-paste. Put a few blanched almonds on the top of each.

Macaroni as Usually Served.

Time, to boil the macaroni, half an hour; to brown it, six or seven minutes.—Take half a pound of pipe macaroni, seven ounces of cheese, four ounces of butter, one pint of new milk, one quart of water and some bread crumbs. Flavor the milk and water with a pinch of salt, set it over the fire, and when boiling drop in the macaroni; when tender, drain it from the milk and water, put it into a deep dish, sprinkle some of the grated cheese amongst it, with part of the butter broken into small pieces, place a layer of grated cheese over the top, and cover the whole with fine bread crumbs, pouring the remainder of the butter lightly warmed over the crumbs; brown the top of the macaroni with a salamander, or before the fire, turning it several times that it may be nicely browned; serve it quickly, and as hot as possible.

Ramakins.

Mix a teaspoonful of flour with two ounces of grated cheese, two ounces of melted butter, two tablespoonfuls of cream, and two well-beaten eggs; stir all well together and bake it in small tins. You may add a little cayenne pepper if you please.

Toasted Cheese.

Cut equal quantities of cheese, and having pared it into extremely small pieces, place it in a pan with a little milk, and a small slice of butter; stir it over a slow fire until melted and quite smooth; take it off the fire quickly, mix the yolk of an egg with it, and brown it in a toaster before the fire.

Welsh Rarebit.

Time, ten minutes.—Take half a pound of cheese, three tablespoonfuls of ale, a thin slice of toast; grate the cheese fine, put it to the ale, and work it in a small saucepan over a slow fire till it is melted; spread it on toast, and send it up boiling hot.

Stewed Apples and Rice.

Peel good baking apples, take out the cores with a scoop so as not to injure the shape of the apples; put them in a deep baking dish and pour over them a syrup made by boiling sugar in the proportion of one pound to a pint of water; put a little piece of shred lemon inside each apple and let them bake very slowly until done, but not in the least broken. If the syrup is thin, boil it until it is thick enough; take out the lemon peel and put a little jam inside each apple, and between them little heaps of well boiled rice. This dish may be served either hot or cold.

BAKING BISCUITS AND CAKES.

General Directions.

An oven to bake well should have a regular heat throughout, but particularly at the bottom, without which bread or cakes will not rise or bake well. An earthen basin is best for beating eggs or cake mixture. Cake should be beaten with a wooden spoon or spatula; butter may be beaten with the same. Eggs should be beaten with rods or a broad fork, a silver fork, or one made of iron wire, is best, as it is broadest. Eggs should be clear and fresh for a cake.

It is well, as a general rule in cake making, to beat the butter and sugar (which must be made fine), to a light cream; indeed, in the making of pound cake the lightness of the cake depends as much upon this as upon the eggs being well beaten; then beat the eggs and put them to the butter, and gradually add the flour and other ingredients, beating it all the time.

In common cakes, where only a few eggs are used, beat them until you can take a spoonful up clear from the strings.

In receipts in which milk is used as one ingredient, either sweet or sour may be used, but not a mixture of both. Sour milk makes a spongy, light cake; sweet milk makes a cake which cuts like pound cake.

To blanch almonds, pour boiling water on them, and let them remain in it until their skins may be taken off; then throw the almonds into cold water to whiten them, drain them from the water, but do not wipe them; the moisture will prevent their oiling.

In making cakes, if you wish them to be pleasing to the palate, use double-refined sugar, although light brown sugar makes a very good cake. For icing cakes, the sugar must be rolled and sifted, or pounded in a mortar.

To ascertain whether a cake is baked enough, if a small one, take a very fine splint of wood and run it through the thickest part; if not done enough, some of the dough or un-baked cake will be found sticking to it; if done, it will come out clean. If the cake is large, pass a small knife blade through it instead of the splint. Cakes to be kept fresh should be placed in a tin box, tightly covered, in a cool, dark place.

Icing for Cakes.

Beat the whites of the eggs to a high froth, then add to them a quarter of a pound of white sugar, pounded and sifted, flavor it with vanilla or lemon, and beat it until it is light and very white, but not quite so stiff as meringue mixture. The longer it is beaten the more firm it will become. Beat it until it may be spread smoothly on the cake.

Feather Cake.

Two cups of sugar, one-half cup of butter, one cup of sweet milk, three cups of flour, three eggs beaten separately, one tea-spoonful of soda, and two of cream of tartar. Flavor with the rind of a fresh lemon. Bake in jelly tins. It is also nice if baked in a loaf and frosted.

Jelly Cake.

Beat three eggs well, the whites and yolks separately; take a cup of fine white sugar and beat that in well with the yolks, and a cupful of sifted flour stirred in gently; then stir in the whites, a little at a time, a teaspoonful of baking powder and one table-spoonful of milk, pour it in three jelly cake plates, and bake from five to ten minutes in a well heated oven, and when cold spread with currant jelly, and place each layer on top of the other and sift powdered sugar on the top.

French Loaf Cake.

Two cups of white sugar, one scant cup of butter, one cup of sweet milk, three heaping cups of flour, three eggs, two teaspoonfuls cream of tartar, one teaspoonful soda. Put sugar, butter, eggs (not previously beaten), soda and cream of tartar all together, beat to a froth; add the milk, beating well, flavor with lemon extract, add the flour gradually, pour into a cake tin lined with buttered paper, sprinkle a little powdered sugar over the cake before baking. It is well to cover it when first putting in the oven, in order not to harden the top too soon.

Marble Cake.

White Part.—Whites of four eggs, one cup white sugar, half cup of butter, half cup sweet milk, two teaspoonfuls of baking powder, one teaspoonful of vanilla or lemons and two and a half cups of sifted flour.

Black Part.—Yolks of four eggs, one cup brown sugar, half cup molasses, half cup butter, half cup sour milk, one teaspoonful soda and one and a half cups sifted flour. Put it in the cake dish alternately, first one part and then the other. The tin should be lined with buttered paper.

Molasses Cake.

Two cupfuls of molasses, one cupful of lard, three-quarters of a cupful of water, one tablespoonful of ginger, three teaspoonfuls of saleratus dissolved, flour enough to make it stiff as pound cake dough.

New Year's Cake.

One pound butter, one and a half pounds sugar, three pounds flour, two tablespoonfuls carraway seed, half a teaspoonful of soda, dissolved in a cupful of milk. Cut long and print, or cut as cookies.

Cocoanut Cake.

Four cups of flour, three of sugar, one cup of milk, five eggs, beaten separately (save the whites of three for icing), one cup of butter, two teaspoonfuls of cream of tartar, one teaspoonful of soda, the half of a cocoanut grated and put into the cake, the other half put with the whites of three eggs and half a cup of powdered sugar, with a little orange water or lemon juice for the icing; bake the cake in jelly pans; when done spread the icing between and on top; put in the oven for a few minutes.

Rich Plum Cake.

Quarter peck finest flour, one pound loaf sugar, three pounds of currants, one pound of raisins, chopped, one-quarter ounce

108

of mace and cloves, a grated nutmeg, peel of a lemon cut fine, half a pound of blanched almonds beaten with rose or orange flower water; mix thoroughly, then melt two pounds of butter in rather more than a pint of cream, put to it a pint of sherry, a glass of brandy, twelve eggs, yolks and white beaten apart, and half a pint of yeast; strain this into the dry ingredients, beat a full hour, butter your hoop, throw in plenty chips of citron, lemon and orange candy, as you put in your batter; bake moderately quickly.

Cream Cakes.

Boil together half a pint of water and two-thirds of a cup of butter; while boiling stir in one and a half cups of flour thoroughly; let it then cool sufficiently, not to cook the eggs, five of which are to be well beaten, and the whole mixed together; drop on tins a spoonful in a place, and bake in a very hot oven, twenty or thirty minutes. It will make two dozen. For the cream boil a pint of new milk, stirring in, beaten together, two eggs with one cup of sugar, and not quite a cup of flour; boil a little, stirring briskly; when cool flavor with lemon; open the cakes at the side with a sharp knife and pour in the cream.

White Mountain Cake.

One pound sugar, one pound flour, half pound butter, six eggs, one large cup of milk, two teaspoonfuls cream of tartar, one of soda, juice of a lemon. Beat yolks and whites together first, then the sugar, beat the butter in a separate dish and then add to the other. Take the milk, divide, and put soda in one-half and cream of tartar in the other; just before you put in the oven put both milks together. Bake one hour; mix the flour in after the butter.

Cocoa Cookies.

Two cups of sugar, one of butter, two eggs, half a grated cocoanut, with flour; roll thin and bake.

Sour Milk Cake.

One cup of sour milk, one cup of sugar, one-half cup of butter, two cups of flour, one egg, one level teaspoonful of soda, half cup of raisins, chopped and spiced to taste.

Fried Cake.

One cup of sugar, one cup of sweet milk, one teaspoonful of cream of tartar, half teaspoonful of soda; add spice to suit the taste; mix in some flour and fry in lard.

Jelly Roll.

Three eggs, one cup of sugar, one teaspoonful of cream of tartar, one-half teaspoonful of soda, one cup of flour; pour it thin into a baking pan; bake slowly; spread jelly over it and roll it up; wrap it in a cloth.

One-Egg Cake.

One and one-third cups of flour, one-third cup of sweet milk, one cup of sugar, one tablespoonful of melted butter, one egg and two tablespoonfuls of baking powder.

Coffee Cake.

One cup brown sugar, one cup molasses, one-half cup each butter and lard, one cup cold coffee, two eggs, one tablespoonful cinnamon, and one of cloves, one grated nutmeg, one teaspoonful soda, flour, one pound each of currants and raisins.

Ginger Cookies.

One cup of sugar, one cup molasses, one cup of lard, two-thirds cup of boiling water, one egg, one teaspoonful cream of tartar, one tablespoonful ginger, one tablespoonful soda, one teaspoonful salt.

Aunt Carrie's Snowflake Cake.

Three eggs, one cup and a half sugar, half cup butter, half cup milk, half teaspoonful of soda, one teaspoonful cream of tartar, two cups flour, whites of two eggs, half cup of sugar, beaten together. Bake in jelly cake tins, frost each layer and sprinkle with grated cocoanut.

Soft Gingerbread.

One tablespoonful butter, one tablespoonful ginger, one-half cup brown sugar, two cups molasses, two cups water or sour milk, one and a half teaspoonfuls soda; do not stir very long; bake in a moderate oven.

Molasses Cookies.

Take two cups of molasses, one cup of sugar, two cups of butter, four teaspoonfuls of alum, put in two cups of boiling water, four teaspoonfuls of soda and flour enough to roll out.

Gelatine Frosting.

One teaspoonful gelatine, two tablespoonfuls of cold water; when the gelatine is soft, one tablespoonful of hot water. When entirely dissolved, add one cup of powdered sugar, and beat it while it is yet warm, until white and light; lemon to taste. This frosts one sheet of cake.

Lemon Cake.

One cup butter, three cups sugar, four cups flour, one cup milk, five eggs, one teaspoonful soda, juice and rind of one lemon.

Newport or Lunch Cake.

One quart sifted flour, two teaspoonfuls of cream of tartar mixed through it, one-half cup of sugar, two eggs, two tablespoonfuls of lard, one cup of sweet milk; lastly dissolve one teaspoonful of soda in a little hot water; mix and bake in a hot oven from twenty to twenty-five minutes.

Scotch Cake.

Flour, one and a half pounds; powdered sugar, three-fourths of a pound; butter, three-fourths of a pound; lard, one-fourth of a pound. Warm your flour and sugar together, then whip butter and lard to a cream, and mix with the flour and sugar. It will be in crumbs which must be pressed together with the hands into small cakes and laid on a paper (without buttering) on a sheet tin. Sprinkle a few comfits on top before baking.

Mother's Raised Biscuit.

Scald one quart of milk; into this, while hot, put a piece of butter the size of an egg; when cold, add one egg, a teacupful of baker's yeast, or home-made; thicken with sifted flour to a batter as thick as muffin batter; let rise, mold, rise again bake quickly.

Fig Cake.

Two cups of sugar, one of butter, one of cold water, with a teaspoonful of soda dissolved in it; three cups of raisins, chopped fine, cinnamon and nutmeg, four eggs, one pound of figs; use the figs whole, covering them well with the cake to prevent burning; bake in layers, frosting between each layer. Make as stiff as pound cake; cut with a very sharp knife to prevent crumbling. This receipt makes two loaves.

Queen's Cake.

One pound of sugar, three-fourths of a pound of butter, eight eggs, beaten separately, one pound of flour, one heaping teaspoonful of baking powder, one wineglass of cherry bounce, two cups of currants.

111

Chocolate Cake.

Two cups of sugar, one-half cup of butter, whites of three eggs, one cup of milk, two and three-fourths cups of flour, three teaspoonfuls of baking powder; bake on jelly tins; whites of two eggs, well beaten, with not quite a cup of pulverized sugar, add six tablespoonfuls of grated German sweet chocolate, and two teaspoonfuls of vanilla; spread the cakes.

Black Cake.

Two pounds of currants, two pounds of raisins (after washing both currants and raisins, when they are dry, dredge with flour), one large spoonful of ground cinnamon, one large spoonful of ground mace, four nutmegs, one gill of molasses, one gill of brandy, one gill of rose water, if you choose; sift one pound of flour into one pan, and one pound of sugar into another, add to the sugar three-quarters of a pound of butter and stir to a cream; beat six eggs light and stir into the butter and sugar alternately with the flour; then add by degrees fruit, spice and liquors, and stir hard; bake in a moderate oven about four hours; let it remain in the oven to cool.

Rice Cake.

One pound of ground rice, one of sugar, half pound of butter, six eggs; flavor with lemon or vanilla, or to suit taste.

Fruit Cake.

One cup of molasses, one pound flour, one of sugar, three-fourths of a pound of butter, two pounds of seeded raisins, three of currants, one of citron, half a pound of blanched almonds, half an ounce of mace, one wineglass brandy, ten eggs; cream the sugar and butter, add the eggs, beaten separately; stir in the flour, brandy, spices and then the fruit.

Strawberry Short Cake.

One quart of flour, sifted, one teaspoonful of salt, two teaspoonfuls of cream of tartar, a piece of butter the size of an egg; rub it in the flour well; dissolve one teaspoonful of soda in a tablespoonful of water, and put the soda water in two cups of milk; bake in a quick oven; take three pints of berries, press half, and then put the other berries in; save some of the juice, and mix some sugar with it; split the cake, butter it, and lay the mixture between. Peaches cut up, sugared, and mixed with a little cream or milk, or oranges cut up, with sugar, and laid between the cake, are also very nice.

Raised Cake.

Three cups of new milk, one cup of yeast, two cups of sugar; work it into a stiff batter with flour, let it rise over night; in the morning put in one and a half cups of butter, one more cup of sugar, one teaspoonful of soda dissolved in milk, put in spices and raisins as long as you can stir it with a spoon.

Cold Water Pound Cake.

Half a cup of butter, two cups of sugar, three eggs, one cup of cold water, three pounds of flour, one teaspoonful cream of tartar, one-half teaspoonful soda.

Orange Cake.

One cup white sugar, one small half cup butter, two cups flour, one-half cup cold water, five eggs—Whites of four only, two teaspoonfuls baking powder, juice and rind of one orange; bake like jelly cake; frost each layer, make frosting of the remaining white.

Cornstarch Cake.

Half pound cornstarch, half pound wheat flour, six eggs, half pound butter, one pound sugar, one small cup sweet milk, two teaspoonfuls baking powder.

Wedding Cake.

One pound of butter, one pound of sugar, nine eggs, one pound of flour, three pounds of currants, two pounds of stoned raisins, one-half teacup of wine or brandy, from one-half to three-quarters pound of citron, one grated nutmeg, some mace and cinnamon; rub the butter and sugar together; when light, add first the yolks and then the whites of the eggs—the yolks and whites of the eggs to be beaten separately—then put in nearly all your flour, keeping out just enough to dust your raisins and cement them; cut your citron in such slices as you like, and put in as you put the cake in the pan; after mixing your fruit in the cake grease a four-quart pan carefully, line it with clean straw paper, a little butter on the paper; put your cake in and bake, in not too quick an oven, for it burns easily. After it is baked take it out of the pan, paper and all, and let it cool. The next day, to keep it fresh and moist, put it back in the pan, or in a tin cake-box, and keep it tightly covered.

Gingerbread Nuts.

One pound of sugar, two pounds of molasses, three-quarters of a pound of butter, four pounds of flour, four ounces of ginger, one ounce of allspice, two spoonfuls of coriander seed, some candied orange peel; two spoonfuls of brandy, yolks of four eggs. Mix the sugar, molasses and butter, and melt all together; then stir in the flour, ground ginger, allspice, coriander seed, and the orange peel, cut very small; mix all into a paste with the eggs well beaten, and the brandy and make them into nuts or cakes.

Ginger Snaps.

Work a quarter of a pound of butter into a pound of fine flour, then mix it with a half pound of molasses, a quarter of a pound brown sugar and one tablespoonful each of ginger and caraway seeds. Work it all well together, and form it into cakes not larger than a crown piece; place them on a baking tin in a moderate oven, when they will be dry and crisp.

Brown Bread Biscuits.

One pound of coarse graham flour, two ounces of butter and a little water. Make the butter and water boiling hot, add it to the flour, keeping it very firm. Roll the biscuits out, not too thin, and bake them in a rather quick oven.

Lemon Biscuits.

Dry well before the fire a pound and a half of flour, rub into it a quarter of a pound of butter as fine as possible, mix with it a pound and a half of loaf sugar, pounded, and the peel of three lemons, chopped very fine. Well beat two eggs, add to them the juice of two lemons, and stir thoroughly. Put the mixture into the flour, and mix all well together, till you have a stiff paste; roll it out to the thickness of a penny piece, and divide it into biscuits with a paste cutter; bake them on a tin. These biscuits should be kept in a tin box near the fire till wanted, as they are apt to give.

Ginger Biscuits.

Eight ounces of flour, four ounces of butter, four ounces of loaf sugar; yolks of three eggs and some ground ginger. Beat the butter to a cream before the fire, add the flour by degrees, then the sugar, pounded and sifted and a flavoring to taste of ground ginger, and mix the whole with the yolks of three well-beaten eggs. When thoroughly mixed, drop the biscuit mixture on buttered paper, a sufficient distance from each other to allow the biscuits to spread, and bake them a light color in a rather slow oven.

114

Plain Biscuits.

One pound of flour, half a pint of milk, two ounces and a half of fresh butter. Dissolve the butter in the milk made warm, but not hot, and stir it into the flour to make a firm paste, roll it out thin with a plain tin shape or a tumbler; prick each biscuit and bake.

PRESERVES AND PICKLES.

Gooseberry Jam.

Three pounds of loaf sugar, six pounds of rough red gooseberries. Pick off .the stalks and buds from the gooseberries and boil them carefully but quickly for rather more than half an hour, stirring continually; then add the sugar pounded fine, and boil the jam quickly for half an hour, stirring it all the time to prevent its sticking to the preserving pan. When done put it into pots, cover it with brandy paper, and secure it closely down with paper moistened with the white of an egg.

To Preserve Cherries.

One pound of sugar to every pound of cherries; and three tablespoonfuls of red currant juice. Lay some pounded sugar at the bottom of the preserving pan, and place some cherries on it, then another layer of sugar, then of cherries, repeating this until all are in, leaving out a little of the sugar to stew in as they boil; add three spoonfuls of currant juice to each pound of fruit, and set it over a clear fire. Boil them quickly, shaking them round frequently to prevent their burning, but do not stir them. Take off the scum as it rises, and when the syrup is thick and they look clear, put them into pots, and when cold, cover them over.

To Bottle Cherries.

Have ready some wide mouthed bottles quite clean and dry; cut each cherry from the stalk into the bottle, be sure not to pull them off. To every bottle of cherries put three ounces of powdered sugar, then tie them tightly over with bladder. After drawing the bread, leave the oven door open. About 9 o'clock at night put in the bottles and close the oven door. Take them out the first thing in the morning and put them in a dry place for use.

Apple Marmalade.

Take a peck of apples, full growth, but not the least ripe, of all or any sort; quarter them and take out the cores, but do not pare them; put them into preserving pan with one gallon of water, and let them boil moderately until you think the pulp will run, or suffer itself to be squeezed through a cheese cloth, only leaving the peels behind. Then to each quart of pulp add one pound, good weight, of loaf sugar, either broken in small pieces or pounded, and boil it all together for half an hour and ten minutes, keeping it stirred; then put it into pots, the larger the better, as it keeps longer in a large body.

Rules to be Observed in Pickling.

Procure always the best vinegar. The success of your pickles depends on the goodness of your vinegar. Use glass bottles for your pickles; if earthen jars, they must be unglazed, as the vinegar acting upon the glaze produces a mineral poison. Use saucepans lined with earthenware, or stone pipkins to boil your vinegar in. If you are compelled to use tin, do not let your vinegar remain in one moment longer than actually necessary. Employ also wooden knives and forks in the preparation of your pickles. Fill the jars three parts full with the articles to be pickled, and then fill the bottle or jar with vinegar. When greening, keep the pickles covered down, as the evaporation of the steam will injure the color.. A little nut of alum may be added to crisp pickles, but it should be very small in proportion to the quantity or it will give a disagreeable flavor.

To Pickle Mushrooms.

Gather some mushroom buttons, wipe them very clean with a piece of flannel dipped in vinegar, then put them into an iron saucepan with pepper, salt, two or three cloves and a very little mace pounded; let them stew over the fire, and after they have produced a great deal of liquor, let them stand by the fire until they have consumed all that liquor up again; but the saucepan must be shaken now and then to prevent their sticking to the bottom. Put them into large nosed bottles, and pour cold vinegar that has been boiled over them, and then cork them up. They will keep for seven years. If the vinegar should dry away, add a little more. Should they be wanted to put over a broiled fowl or veal cutlets, take a few out of the bottle and pour some boiling water over them to take off the sourness, then put them immediately over the cutlets.

116

To Pickle Onions.

Take some nice onions, peel and throw them into a stew-pan of boiling water; set them over the fire, and let them remain until quite clear; then take them out quickly, and lay them between two cloths to dry. Boil some vinegar with the ginger and whole pepper, and when cold pour it over the onions in glass jars, and tie them closely over.

Pickled Peaches.

Nine pounds peaches, three pounds sugar, three quarts good cider vinegar. Peel the peaches, put two cloves in each peach, then put them with the sugar and vinegar in a porcelain lined kettle; cook from five to ten minutes. Add a little whole allspice.

Sweet Tomato Pickles.

Eight pounds peeled tomatoes, four of powdered sugar, cinnamon, cloves and allspice, each one ounce. Boil one hour, and then add a quart of boiling vinegar.

Pickled Cucumbers.

To a gallon of water add a quart of salt, put in the cucumbers, and let them stay over night. In the morning wash them out of the brine and put them carefully into a stone jar. Boil a gallon of vinegar, put it in while cold, quarter of a pound of cloves, and a tablespoonful of alum; when it boils hard skim it well and turn over the cucumbers. In a week they will be fit for use.

Green Pickles for Daily Use.

A gallon of vinegar, three-quarters of a pound of salt, quarter pound of ginger, an ounce of mace, quarter ounce of cayenne pepper, and an ounce of mustard seed, simmered in vinegar, and when cold put in a jar. You may throw in fresh vegetables when you choose.

Tomato Soy.

To one peck of grene tomatoes, sliced thin, add one pint of salt; stand twenty-four hours; strain, and put on the fire with twelve raw onions, an ounce of black pepper, one ounce of allspice, quarter of a pound of ground mustard, half a pound of white mustard seed, and a little cayenne pepper. Cover with vinegar and boil till as thick as jam, stirring occasionally with a wooden spoon, to prevent burning.

Mock Capers.

Take green nasturium seeds when they are full grown, but not yellow; dry for a day in the sun; then put them in jars and cover with boiling vinegar, spiced, and when cool cork closely. Fit for use in six weeks.

Pepper Catsup.

Fifty pods of large red peppers, with the seeds. Add a pint of vinegar, and boil until the pulp will mash through a sieve. Add to the pulp a second pint of vinegar, two spoonfuls of sugar, cloves, mace spice, onions and salt. Put all in a kettle, and boil to a proper consistency.

Pickled Red Cabbage.

Cut the cabbage in thin slices, spread it on a sieve and sprinkle it with salt; let it drain for twenty-four hours, dry it, pack it in pickle jars, fill them with cold vinegar, put in spice to taste, and tie the jars up firmly. Open the jars in a few days and if the cabbage has shrunk, fill up with vinegar.

Pickled Green Tomatoes.

Let the tomatoes stand in salt and water for twelve hours. Then stick four or five cloves in each one, and pour boiling vinegar over them. Place them in a jar and set them in a cool place.

Spiced Currants.

Five pounds of currants, two pounds sugar, one pint vinegar, one tablespoonful each of salt, pepper, cinnamon and cloves, mash well together and boil twenty minutes.

Tomato Catsup.

Cut the tomatoes in two and boil for half an hour, then press through a hair sieve and add spices in the proportion given below, after which boil for about three hours over a slow fire. Remove from the fire, turn it out, and let it stand till next day, when you must add half a pint of vinegar for each peck of tomatoes. For every like amount of the vegetable, add, while boiling, one-eighth of an ounce of red and one-quarter of an ounce of black pepper, half an ounce each of mace, allspice and cloves, and two ounces of mustard—all finely powdered. Salt to suit, and put in a little ginger, and essence of celery, if you so desire. Bottle, seal the corks and keep in a dark place.

Pickled Pears.

Ten pounds of pears, three pounds of light brown sugar, one quart of vinegar, one ounce of cinnamon, one ounce of cloves (ground), one-quarter pound of citron; put all in together and boil until the pears are tender, skim the pears out and let the syrup boil half an hour longer.

French Mustard.

Take a quarter of a pound of best yellow mustard, pour over it half a pint each of water and vinegar. Add a pinch of salt and a piece of calamus root the size of a pea. Put it on the fire and when it boils add a tablespoonful of flour, let it boil twenty minutes, stirring it constantly. Just before taking it off stir in a teaspoonful of sugar or honey. When cool, put it into bottles and cork tightly.

Chow-Chow.

A peck of tomatoes, two quarts of green peppers, half a peck of onions, two cabbages cut as for slaw, and two quarts of mustard seed. Have a large firkin, put in a layer of sliced tomatoes, then one of onions; next one of peppers, lastly cabbage; sprinkle over some of the mustard seed, repeat the layers again and so on until you have used up the above quantity. Boil a gallon of vinegar with a bit of alum, two ounces of cloves and two of allspice tied in a little bag and boiled with the vinegar, skim it well and turn into the firkin. Let it stand twenty-four hours, then pour the whole into a large kettle and let it boil five minutes; turn into the firkin and stand away for future use.

Preserved Apples.

Core and pare a dozen good-sized apples, and cut into eighths, make a syrup of a pound of sugar to half a pint of water; let it boil, and then put in as much apple as can be boiled without breaking; remove them carefully when tender; after all are done, add a little more sugar, boil a few minutes, flavor with lemon and pour over the apples.

Preserved Pineapple.

A pound of sugar to a pound of pineapple; put the slices in water, and boil a quarter of an hour; then remove them and add the sugar to the water; put in the apple and boil fifteen minutes. Boil the syrup till thick.

Apple Jam.

Core and pare a good quantity of apples, chop them well, allow equal weight of apples and sugar, make a syrup of your sugar by adding a little water, boiling and skimming well, then throw in some grated lemon peel and a little white ginger with the apples; boil until the fruit looks clear.

Green Gage Jam.

Rub rips green gages through a sieve, put all the pulp into a pan with an equal weight of loaf sugar pounded and sifted. Boil the whole till sufficiently thick, and put into pots.

Preserved Lemon Peel.

Make a thick syrup of white sugar, chop the lemon peel fine and boil it in the syrup ten minutes; put in glass tumblers and paste paper over. A teaspoonful of this makes a loaf of cake, or a dish of sauce nice.

To Crystalize Fruit.

Pick out the finest of any kind of fruit, leave on their stalks, beat the whites of three eggs to a stiff froth, lay the fruit in the beaten egg with the stalks upward, drain them and beat the part that drips off again, select them out one by one and dip them into a cup of finely powdered sugar, cover a pan with a sheet of fine paper, place the fruit inside of it and put it in an over that is cooling; when the icing on the fruit becomes firm pile them on a dish and set them in a cool place.

Preserved Tomatoes.

A pound of sugar to a pound of tomatoes. Take six pounds of each; the peel and puice of four lemons and a quarter of a pound of ginger tied up in a bag; put on the side of the range and boil slowly for three hours.

Cider Apple Sauce.

Take a porcelain lined kettle, fill it with rich, sweet cider, boil more than half way, then empty into stone pot. Have ready sweet apples, pared and quartered, fill the kettle with them, pour on part of the cider, cover and let them stew until the apples are done, add the rest of the cider and a little sugar, and stir until quite thick. It is better to boil it several hours, as the longer it is boiled the longer it can be kept; while boiling add spice to taste.

Preserved Strawberries.

Pick off all the stems, and to very quart of fruit add a quart of sugar; mix well with the sugar and put them over a slow fire

120

till the syrup commences to form, then put them over a hot fire and let them boil quickly for fifteen minutes, skimming it well. Put them boiling hot into stone jars, seal up tightly.

To Preserve Green Gooseberries Whole.

To one pound of gooseberries allow one pound and a half of double refined sugar, and one pint and a half of water. Pick off the black eye, but not the stalk, from the largest green gooseberries you can procure, and set them over the fire to scald, taking care they do not boil. When they are tender, take them out, and put them into cold water. Then clarify a pound and a half of sugar in a pint and a half of water, and when the syrup is cold put the gooseberries singly into your preserving pan, add the syrup, and set them over a gentle fire. Let them boil slowly, but not quick enough to break them. When you perceive the sugar has entered them, take them off, cover them with white paper and let them stand all night. The next day take out the fruit and boil the syrup until it begins to be ropy. Skim it well, add it to the gooseberries, and set them over a slow fire to simmer till the syrup is thick. Then take them out. Set them to cool, and put them with the syrup into pots. Cover them over, and keep them in a dray place.

Strawberry Jam.

To six pounds of strawberries allow three pounds of sugar. Procure some fine scarlet strawberries, strip off the stalks and put them into preserving pan over a moderate fire, boil them for half an hour, keeping them constantly stirred. Break the sugar into small pieces and mix them with the strawberries after they have been removed from the fire. Then place it again over the fire, and boil it for another half an hour very quickly. Put it into pots, and when cold cover it over with brandy papers and a piece of paper moistened with the white of an egg over the tops.

Raspberry Jam.

To every pound of raspberries use the same weight of sugar, but always boil the fruit well before you add the sugar to it, as that will make it a better color. Put the fruit in a preserving pan, mashing it well with a long wooden spoon. After boiling it a few minutes, add the same quantity of sugar as fruit, boiling it half an hour, keeping it well stirred. When done, and sufficiently reduced, fill the jars, and when cold ocver them over with white paper moistened with white of an egg.

Rhubarb Marmalade.

To one pound of loaf sugar, one pound and a half of rhubarb stalks, peel of half a large lemon, a quarter of an ounce of bitter almonds.

Cut the rhubarb stalks into pieces about two inches long and put them into a preserving pan with the loaf sugar broken small, the peel of the lemon cut thin, and the almonds blanched and divided. Boil the whole well together, put it into pots and cover it as directed for other preserves.

To Preserve Plums.

To every pound of fruit allow three-quarters of a pound of sugar. Divide the plums, take out the stones, and put the fruit on a dish with pounded sugar strewed over; the next day put them into a preserving pan and let them simmer gently by the side of the fire for about thirty minutes, then boil them quickly, removing the scum as it rises, and keep them constantly stirred, or the jam will stick to the bottom of the pan. Crack the stones and add the kernels to the preserve when it boils.

To Preserve Lettuce Stalks.

Cut into pieces of about three inches in length some stalks of large lettuce, and soak them in cold water for ten minutes, washing them very clean. Put a pound and a half of sugar into a preserving pan with six pints of water and three large dessertspoonfuls of ground ginger. Set it over a clear fire to boil for twenty-five minutes, then pour it into a deep dish to remain all night. The next day repeat the boiling for half an hour; do this for five or six days, and then drain them free from moisture on a sieve reversed. Make a rich syrup of sugar, water, and three ounces of whole ginger, just bruised; put the lettuce again into a preserving pan, pour the syrup over them, and boil them several times until the stalks become clear, taking care the syrup is sufficiently strong of the ginger.

Blackberry Jam.

Crush a quart of fully ripe blackberries with a pound of the best loaf sugar pounded very fine, put it into a preserving pan, and set it over a gentle fire until thick, add a glass of brandy, and stir it again over the fire for about a quarter of an hour; then put it into pots and when cold tie them over.

Black Currant Jam.

Gather the currants when they are thoroughly ripe and dry, and pick them from the stalks. Bruise them lightly in a large

122

bowl, and to every pound of fruit put three-quarters of a pound of finely beaten loaf sugar; put the sugar and fruit into a preserving pan and boil them from three-quarters to one hour, skimming as the scum rises, and stirring constantly; then put the jam into pots, cover them with brandy paper, and tie them closely over.

Black Currant Jelly.

Gather the currants when ripe, on a dry day, strip them from the stalks and put them into an earthen pan or jar, and to every five quarts allow a half pint of water; tie the pan over and set it in the oven for an hour and a quarter, then squeeze out the juice through a coarse cloth, and to every pint of juice put a pound of loaf sugar, broken into pieces; boil it for three-quarters of an hour, skimming it well; then pour it into small pots, and when cold put brandy papers over them and tie them closely over.

Red Currant Jelly.

Pick the currants from the stalks into a broad earthenware pan. To about one gallon of the picked currants put half a pound of sifted lump sugar. Put the sugar over the picked currants the day before you make the jelly. Set the currants over a slow fire to simmer gently for about twenty minutes, the slower they simmer the greater quantity of juice they will discharge. There should be an equal quantity of red and white currants. When all the juice is discharged, strain it through a hair sieve, and then through a jelly bag while quite hot. Now to each quart of juice put one pound of powdered loaf sugar. Put it into a preserving pan, and set it over a quick stove to boil for twenty minutes. If any scum rises, skim it off. When done, put it into small white pots or little glasses, and cover it with brandied paper. Tie down.

Orange Marmalade.

Take six pounds of oranges; cut the peel so as to make it peel off in four pieces. Put all the peels on the fire in a preserving pan, with a large quantity of water, and boil them for two hours, then cut them in very thin slices. While they are boiling press the inside of the oranges through a splinter sieve, narrow enough to prevent the seeds and skin from going through. When this is done, and the peels cut into the thinnest shreds, put the whole on a fire in a copper or brass pan, with eight pounds of loaf sugar broken small. Boil it all together for ten minutes ; it may then be taken off the fire and put into preserving jars.

HINTS TO HOUSEWIVES.

How to Choose Meat, Fish, Poultry, Etc.

We advise housewives to market for themselves; but as some skill is required in a purchaser (if this duty is to be performed to advantage), we will endeavor to give directions by which inexperienced housewives may be enabled to select good articles.

First in the list comes butcher's meat; of which beef is considered the best by most people. An ox should be kept five or six years before it is killed; it is then in its prime. Ox-beef is the best. It is a fine grained meat; the lean of a bright red color, intermingled with grains of fat, when it is well fed and good. The fat should be white, not yellow, and the suet also white and firm. Beef should never be lean; it is tough and bad unless there is a good quantity of fat. Heifer beef is paler than ox beef, and closer grained; the fat whiter, and the bones, of course, smaller. Bull beef is only described to be avoided. It is dark colored and coarse grained; has very little fat, and a strong meaty smell about it.

Of these joints, choose the rib or sirloin for roasting. If you purchase ribs of beef, let them be the middle ribs. You may have one, two, three or four ribs, as you will; but one rib is too thin to be economical, as it dries up in cooking. If, however, your family be small, a single rib, with the bones taken out, rolled, and stuffed will make a nice little roast. If you buy a sirloin, take care to have it cut from the thin end, which has a good under cut or fillet, as then, in addition to a roast joint, you will have another dish, a fillet of beef, one of the best dishes ever served.

The rump is preferred to the sirloin by epicures, but it is too large to be served whole. A sufficiently large joint is cut from the thin end to roast.

For dinner for a large family, where economy is essential, the buttock of beef is excellent, and very profitable. It is cheaper than the other roasting portions of the ox, has no bones. and affords quantities of rich gravy. But it should be hung for some time until quite tender. The round, aitchbone and silverside are usually salted and boiled. The neck is used for making soup or gravy—ask for it as "gravy beef," the thin flank is the part to be collared. A "rump steak" is to be ordered for frying, etc. A "beefsteak" does for stewing, puddings, pies, etc. The inferior and cheaper parts of beef make excellent soup.

124

Veal should be small and white, and the kidney well covered with fat. The flesh should be dry, closely grained and white; if it is moist and clammy it is stale, and not fit for cooking.

The fillet, loin, shoulder and best end of the neck are the roasting joints. The breast is sometimes roasted in very small families, but it is usually stewed, as is also the knuckle; or the knuckle may be boiled, and served with parsley and butter; a calf's head is a delicacy. Calf's feet are also valuable boiled, stewed or used for jelly. Veal makes the best stock for rich soups and gravies. It is a most useful meat for made dishes of all kinds, on account of its delicate flavor.

Mutton.—Wether mutton is best. It may be known by its having a knob of fat on the upper part of the leg. It should be dark colored and have plenty of fat. The color is important, as it is a proof of age, and the older mutton is the better it is. All the joints of a sheep may be roasted. The saddle is the best. The haunch is next best to the saddle; it is the leg and loin undivided. The leg and neck are frequently boiled. The leg and loin separated are the best joints after the haunch. Chops are cut from the loin; cutlets from the thick end of the loin, best end of the neck, or middle of the leg. The leg is sometimes cured and smoked as a ham. The breast of mutton is often salted and boiled. The scrag end of mutton is very good stewed with rice.

Lamb should be small, of a pale colored red, and fat. Lamb is generally roasted. The leg of "house lamb" (which is in season just before Christmas) is sometimes boiled and served with white sauce.

Venison.—You can tell as to being "high" or not, by running a skewer into the shoulder and observing the scent on it when withdrawn. The fat should be thick and clean. If the cleft of the haunch is smooth and close, the animal is young.

Pork.—The fat of pork should be firm, and the lean white and finely grained. The rind or skin thin and smooth. If the flesh feels clammy to the touch the pork is bad; if the fat has kernels in it the pig has been measly, and the meat should not be eaten. Pork should be perfectly sweet to be good, therfore, do not hang it long.

Bacon.—If bacon is good the rind is thin, the fat firm and pinkish, the lean tender and adhering to the bone. Rusty bacon has yellowish streaks in it.

Hams are tried by sticking a knife or skewer into them up to the knuckle, if when drawn out it has a nice smell, the ham is good. A bad scent will be perceived if it is tainted.

The roasting joints of pork are the spare rib, loin and the leg, the other joints are salted; the leg may also be cured and boiled. The sides or flitches are made into bacon. The leg makes a ham.

Meat should be wiped with a dry cloth as soon as it comes from the butcher's flyblows should be cut out, and in loins, the long pipe that runs by the bone should be taken out as it soon taints; the kernels also should be removed from beef. Never receive bruised joints. If you wish to keep your meat hanging longer than ordinary, dredge it well with pepper. Powdered charcoal dusted over it will also prevent its tainting, nay, will absolutely remove the taint from meat already gone; we have seen a pair of fowls quite green from unavoidable long keeping, made fresh and sweet as ever by being sprinkled with powdered charcoal for an hour before dressing. In hot summers it is advisable to keep a lunmp of charcoal in the larder. Meat becomes more digestable and tender by hanging, but lamb and veal cannot be kept so well as beef and mutton.

To Choose Poultry and Game.

Turkey.—The cock bird, when young, has a smooth black leg with a short spur. The eyes are bright and full, and the feet supple, when fresh; the absence of these signs denotes age and staleness; the hen may be judged by the same rules.

Fowls.—The young rooster has a smooth leg and a short spur, when fresh the vent is close and dark. Hens, when young, have smooth legs and combs; when old, these will be rough; a good capon has a thick belly and large rump, a poll comb and a swelling breast.

Geese.—In young geese the feet and bills will be yellow and free from hair. When fresh the feet are pliable; they are stiff when stale.

Ducks may be selected by the same rules.

Pigeons, when fresh, have supple feet, and the vent will be firm; if discolored they are stale.

Rabbits.—When a rabbit is young and fresh, the cleft in the lip is narrow, the body stiff, and the claws are smooth and sharp; old and stale ones will be the opposite of this.

To Choose Eggs.

Shake the eggs; if they are bad they will rattle. But we think the best plan is to put them in a basin of water, and see if they lie on their side, down in it. If the egg turns upon its end it is bad; if it lies obliquely, it is not quite fresh, but may do for puddings, etc.

126

A happy home,
A smiling wife,
A meal cooked right,
Ah, that is life!

FOR ADVANCED PUPILS.
CANDY FOR THE CHILDREN.
Maple Caramels.

One pound sugar, one-half pound maple sugar, one-half pint rich cream. Heat slowly and when it begins to boil, add two tablespoonfuls butter and one-quarter teaspoonful cream of tartar; cook slowly until it snaps in cold water. Pour on buttered tins and mark in squares while warm.

Ice Cream Taffy.

Two cups sugar, one tablespoonful of butter, enough water to dissolve the sugar. Boil eight minutes. Add one-half teaspoonful of cream of tartar and boil seven minutes longer. Take from the fire and add one teaspoonful of vanilla extract and pull until white.

Chocolate Caramels.

Take of grated chocolate, milk, sugar, molasses, one cupful of each, piece of butter the size of an egg; boil until it drops hard; pour on buttered dish and before it cools mark off into square blocks.

Butter Scotch.

Five tablespoonfuls molasses, four tablespoonfuls sugar, four tablespoonfuls water, two tablespoonfuls butter; let boil until when dropping a little in cold water it will be brittle. Put in a pinch of soda before taking off the stove, pour on buttered tins and when cool enough, mark in squares.

Cocoanut Caramels.

Two cups sugar, with enough water to boil it. When ready to take off the stove, put in one cup of cocoanut, with a piece of butter. Flavor with vanilla.

Chocolate Fudge.

Two cups sugar, two-thirds cup of milk and butter size of a walnut. Put on the stove and when it comes to a boil add one square of chocolate, grated. When done remove from fire and add one teaspoonful of vanilla and stir with a spoon until it thickens. Then pour on buttered tins and when cool enough mark in squares.

THIS IS A JOKE—DON'T USE THE RECEIPT.

Question.

Dear Editor:—How do you make peach marmalade?

NEWLY WED.

Answer.

Peach marmalade: Take four able-bodied peaches, soak in vinegar until mellow; then add four ounces of baking powder and Worcestershire sauce to taste. Bake over a slow fire until thoroughly done. Serve hot with lettuce and bay rum. This is original.

CPSIA information can be obtained
at www.ICGtesting.com
Printed in the USA
JSHW040533011022
31213JS00001B/26